DENBY
STONEWARES
A Collector's Guide

FRONTISPIECE. *A display of Electric Blue pieces*

DENBY
STONEWARES

A Collector's Guide

Graham and Alva Key

EMS AND ENS LTD

First published October 1995

ISBN 1-874558-03-5

Published by
Ems and Ens Ltd, Stapleton House, Langtree,
Torrington, Devon EX38 8NP

Printed in Great Britain by
Chichester Press Ltd, Chichester,
West Sussex PO19 2UW

Acknowledgements

W E would like to offer our special thanks to the following people, without whose assistance, advice and encouragement this book would not have been possible: Dena Annable; Nora Beardsley; Glyn Colledge; Richard Gamester; Mr Hallam; Richard Halliwell; Ziggy and Stella Kapera; Ronald and Dorothy Key; Clare Lewis; John Lingard; Bill Loram; Audrey Machin (née Jackson); Terry and Diana Millner; Lin Salt; Tim Searcy; Jill and Clare Sellars; Peter Sharp; Douglas Stone; Anne and Peter Swan; Shirley Vallance; Beverley Walters; Eileen White; Joan and Jef Whitham; Mrs Wood; Phil Yates and Maggie France. We would also like to acknowledge the help of the Victoria & Albert Museum; Mellors & Kirk, Nottingham; and the Hanley Library, Stoke-on-Trent.

We are also indebted to Trevor Hillman for his photographic work, and to Alan Slater for his illustrative work. Our thanks must also go to the following organisations and people for kindly allowing us to reproduce photographic material for which they own the copyright: Denby Pottery Company Limited (Figures 2, 115, 121 and 145); Mellors & Kirk, Nottingham (Figure 50); Richard Gamester (Figures 102 and 117, and Plates 46 and 55).

In preparing the text we have consulted a number of sources of reference and we would like to acknowledge our indebtedness to the following books and journals: *Browne Muggs (English Brown Stoneware)*, ROBIN HILDYARD, Victoria & Albert Museum; *Torquay Motto Wares*, ed. VIRGINIA BRISCO, Torquay Pottery Collectors' Society; *Stoneware Bottles (1500–1949)*, DEREK ASKEY, Bowman Graphics; *Ceramics (Twentieth Century Design)*, FRANCES HANNAH, E P Dutton; *Doulton Ink Wares*, COLIN ROBERTS, Bee Publications; *Encyclopaedia of British Art Pottery*, VICTORIA BERGESEN, Barrie & Jenkins; *English Brown Stoneware (1670–1900)*, ADRIAN OSWALD, R J C HILDYARD & R G HUGHES, Faber & Faber; *The Ceramic Art of Great Britain*, LLEWELLYNN JEWITT, New Orchard Editions; *Stoneware Hot Water Bottles*, J SPEARING; *Buying Antique Pottery & Porcelain*, RACHEL FEILD, Macdonald; *Wemyss Ware – The Devonshire Years*, B ADAMS, D THORN & E WEEKES, B & T Thorn and Son; *The Ewenny Potteries*, J M LEWIS, National Museum of Wales; *Pottery Gazette*, 1878–1918; *Pottery Gazette and Glass Trade Review*, 1919–1970; Arts and Crafts Exhibition Society catalogues.

Foreword

DESPITE the fact that Denby Pottery has been a steadfast name in English ceramics since its formation in 1809, relatively little has been written about its wares. This reference work, which is the first definitive guide of its kind, will prove essential reading for the increasing number of Denby antique enthusiasts.

The authors have spent twenty years recording the diverse range of products manufactured by Denby Pottery over the decades, from the rugged stoneware bottles and jars of the early 19th century to the distinctive and highly acclaimed tableware designs of the 1950s and 1960s. It is through their efforts that the antique market now has a better understanding of Denby Pottery's wares.

Graham and Alva Key are well known to members of the Denby Collectors' Club; their regular 'Collectables' column is popular with both experienced collectors and those recently acquainted with Denby. In this volume they share their extensive knowledge and enthusiasm for the pottery which has played a large part in their lives.

Stephen Riley
Managing Director
The Denby Pottery Company Limited

Contents

Colour Illustrations

Introduction

THE name Denby is very close to our home and to our hearts, as we were born and bred virtually within sight of the Pottery; we remember from our childhood, the Marmaduke Rabbit doorstop and the small Electric Blue Trumpet vase filled with spills on our grandparents' mantelpiece.

Our interest in Denby Stonewares was nurtured from the time we met, and has continued throughout our married life; it seemed only natural that two people living and working away from their native Derbyshire should begin collecting artefacts which reminded them of home. On our first visit to a local village auction in rural Leicestershire, some twenty years ago, we purchased a box of 'odds' which contained a vase of Electric Blue glaze, and this 'find' set us on course for what has proved to be a fascinating and absorbing leisure time pursuit, and ultimately a business.

To many people, Denby pots are the plates, cups, teapots and cookware that are used in the day-to-day ritual of eating meals. However, few people realise what an interesting and varied history the Pottery has. Our pursuit of old Denby has taken us to every corner of the country, visiting hundreds of antiques fairs, centres, shops and markets, and the constant handling of the pieces has developed in us an appreciation of Derbyshire stoneware. Although over the years we accumulated a wealth of information about Denby, it was evident that little had been written about the Pottery and its products. So, in response to the ever-increasing number of collectors, together with the encouragement of the Pottery, we decided to put pen to paper and write the first book on Denby stonewares.

Having decided to write the book we then began ensuring that the information already to hand was correct, as well as obtaining the information that was still required. During this time, we have met many fellow admirers of the excellent workmanship and originality of style that have come from the Denby Pottery over the years, and we have been truly grateful for the generosity of some of these collectors, for access to entire collections for comparison, admiration and for photographic purposes.

We have been aware, at auctions and antiques fairs, of the growing stature of decorative stoneware produced at Denby and this is partly due to the recognition and appreciation of the design skills of Glyn Colledge and his father, Albert. On the visits we have made to see Glyn, he has been most welcoming and has shared with us his expert knowledge and anecdotal information from his long service at the Pottery.

We have also been welcomed by a number of retired Denby employees who have given us invaluable information concerning obscure pottery designs, pottery marks, and turners and figuremen's marks; we have also been delighted by their fondness for the factory and charmed by their many humorous anecdotes.

We would like to thank the Denby Pottery Company Limited for their generosity in allowing us unlimited access to archive material, privileged handling of their museum exhibits, and for the facility of photographing on their premises. We are particularly indebted to Linda Salt, their public relations officer, without whose help, guidance, encouragement and friendship, this book could not have been written. Her own love of the stonewares and her singular knowledge and experience of Denby, both past and present, has been shared with us throughout our lengthy research.

We have been privileged in sharing our appreciation of old Denby with Tim Searcy, whose joy and delight in the Denby Stonewares arises from his own – and his family's – long association with Joseph and Florence Bourne-Wheeler, who were the owners of the Pottery in the 1930s when the production of decorative art wares was at its height. We are honoured that such a fine artist, now enjoying the peace and tranquillity of his Derbyshire home, designed the cover of *Denby Stonewares* for us.

This book – although not a comprehensive catalogue of the whole range of Denby Stonewares produced at the Denby, Belper and Codnor Park potteries – will provide guidance on the availability, identification and appreciation of the wide variety of domestic and decorative wares produced over almost 200 years. Being the first definitive book on Denby collectables we have included an illustrated glossary of incised and underglazed pottery marks with approximate dates when each was in use.

A comprehensive record has not been preserved of the entire range of Denby Stonewares, but it is hoped that the information we have gathered through our collecting and research over the last twenty years, together with the invaluable assistance of the Denby Pottery Company Limited themselves, will prove of interest and help to both the casual browser and the enthusiastic collector.

Graham and Alva Key
October 1995

1

A Brief History of the Pottery

DERBYSHIRE is a county with a long and famous pedigree in the manufacturing of stoneware pottery. Denby itself is only some fourteen miles from Nottingham which, in the 17th century, was second only to London in the production of salt-glazed stoneware pottery. Contemporary with the pottery manufacture at Nottingham was a small potmaking establishment at the village of Crich, in the Peak District foothills (only some six miles away from Denby). This pottery, founded around 1700, produced salt-glazed wares similar to those from Nottingham.

In the north of the county, in the Chesterfield area, the Brampton and Whittington Moor potteries were particularly important, and the stoneware produced there during the late 18th and early 19th centuries is now highly collectable and much sought-after. Also, in the late 18th and early 19th centuries, there were important potteries south of Derby in the Melbourne and Hartshorne locality.

Turning back to the immediate locality around Denby itself, apart from Crich, many other small towns and villages had their own potmaking works – these included Alfreton, Belper, Eastwood, Shipley, Codnor Park, Ilkeston and Langley Mill. Figure 1 shows the location of the various stoneware potteries in Derbyshire in the 18th and 19th centuries.

The reason why, historically, Derbyshire was one of the country's major producers of stoneware pottery can be closely associated with the geology of the region. Derbyshire was, until the 1970s, an extensive coal-mining area, and large quantities of rich clay (sometimes red in colour due to deposits of iron) are found in close proximity (geologically) to the coal measures; it is this clay which is particularly suitable for the making of stoneware pottery.

It was deposits of clay such as these which were found at Denby in 1806, on land owned by William Drury-Lowe of Locko Park near Derby, when the turnpike road was constructed from Derby to Alfreton, and which sufficiently interested a certain Mr Jager to build a potworks on the site in 1809; this clay, incidentally, is still mined in the locality for the production of modern Denby tableware, and was, for a time, supplied to Derby China Works for the making of saggars.

The year 1812 was very important in the history of Denby Pottery, for it was then that Joseph Bourne took over the works from Mr Jager. Historically, around

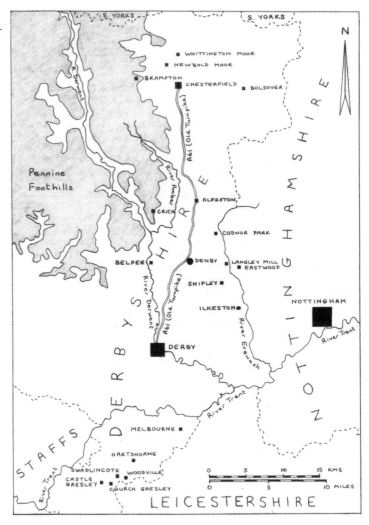

Figure 1.
The locations of
the Derbyshire
stoneware
potteries

the turn of the century, there were many potters with the surname Bourne, many of whom appear to be related to Joseph Bourne. He was the youngest of four potter sons of William Bourne, who owned the pottery in the neighbouring town of Belper (about four miles away from Denby). The eldest son, William (jnr), was a partner in the Nile Street, Burslem, pottery of Pinder, Bourne and Co. (which was later bought by Doulton of Lambeth), and he later went on to purchase the pottery at Church Gresley in south Derbyshire, and this was eventually sold to a Mr T G Green, under whose name it still operates today. Work at the Belper and Denby Potteries was carried on simultaneously until, in 1834, the Belper Pottery was closed and the workforce transferred to the newly enlarged Denby site. The Bourne family also had interests in other local potteries – they took over the Codnor Park Pottery in 1833 from William Burton, and the Shipley Pottery circa 1845. However, by the year 1861, both of these potteries had closed too and the workforces also transferred to Denby.

By this time, the Denby plant had been considerably enlarged, and changes had been made in the size and form of the salt-glazing kilns. The improvements were patented by Joseph Bourne and the quality of the stoneware produced inevitably enhanced the company's already high reputation.

In 1841, the firm became known as Joseph Bourne and Son, the son being Joseph Harvey Bourne (the only one of four sons to survive into adulthood). This son, born in 1819, continued to run the pottery after the death of his father, Joseph, in 1860, at the age of 72. However, Joseph Harvey Bourne himself died at the premature age of 49 in 1869, and his widow, Sarah Elizabeth Bourne, became the sole proprietor of the Denby Pottery for the next thirty years. It seems, by all accounts, that she was a very capable and competent business-woman, and the factory continued to prosper under her guidance; the workforce during this time had increased to around 400, including 90 throwers, and the range of products was considerably extended to include decorated art ware and oven ware with coloured glazes.

Unfortunately, Joseph Harvey and Sarah Elizabeth had no children to inherit the business, so, upon Sarah Elizabeth's death in 1898, she was succeeded by a partnership of two of her nephews, Joseph Bourne-Wheeler and Joseph Henry Topham. The former of these was left as sole proprietor in 1907 when Mr Topham withdrew from the business. Joseph Bourne-Wheeler remained active in the company, mainly as governing director, until his death in 1942 at the age of 86.

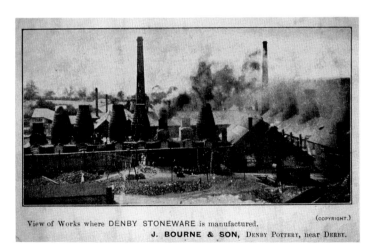

View of Works where DENBY STONEWARE is manufactured. (COPYRIGHT.)
J. BOURNE & SON, DENBY POTTERY, near DERBY.

Figure 2.
View of the
Denby Pottery,
circa 1900

15

In 1909 (the year of Denby Pottery's centenary), Joseph Bourne-Wheeler was responsible for the expansion of the factory, which included the building of new warehouses and the installation of new kilns and ovens to cope with the enormous output. He also successfully saw Denby Pottery formed into a limited liability company in 1916.

Following the General Strike of 1926 and the subsequent Depression, the future for Denby Pottery in 1930 looked decidedly bleak. It was at this time that Norman Wood joined the management, and, supported by John Dale (the fourth generation of the Dale family to work with the company), they were instrumental in dispensing with the old, inefficient salt-glazing kilns and were responsible for the installation of Dressler tunnel kilns as well as attracting the first free-lance designers to the pottery.

In this period leading up to World War II, there was an increase in the production and popularity of decorative stoneware, as well as an expansion and development of domestic ware. After the restrictions of the war years, in the late 1940s and early 1950s, the father and son designing team of Albert and Glyn Colledge introduced the country's first hand-decorated domestic designs in stoneware, and also a range of hand-glazed and decorated art wares which were to remain popular for some twenty years.

The nearby stoneware-producing pottery at Langley Mill, on the Derbyshire and Nottinghamshire border, was acquired by Denby in 1959, and in 1970, the Denby Pottery shares were floated on the stock market. By 1976, the name Joseph Bourne and Son had disappeared, and the factory became known as Denby Tableware Limited. Crown House plc took over the pottery in 1981, which resulted in the eventual closure of the Langley Mill Pottery in 1982 and the transference of plant and workforce to the Denby site.

Refurbishment and installation of new kilns followed the acquisition of Denby Pottery by the Coloroll Group in 1987, but in 1990, as a result of the business being purchased by the management, Denby became re-established as an independent pottery once more and traded as the Denby Pottery Company Limited. In June 1994, to further expand the business, Denby was floated on the London Stock Exchange.

2

Nineteenth-Century Wares

ALTHOUGH fashions may change and tastes may alter, pottery reflects the spirit of the age, and in Victorian times the majority of the wares produced by Joseph Bourne at Denby were for the retailing of consumables in bottles and jars of every shape and size. However, the craftsmen at the pottery were highly skilled and produced some very fine examples of decorative and commemorative salt-glazed stoneware. If you have visited the Denby Pottery Museum, you cannot fail to have admired the much-photographed Wesley Centenary Bowl, made in 1839 (Figure 3). The Bourne family were very strong Methodists and at least two local chapels were founded by William Bourne and his son Joseph.

Figure 3. Wesley Centenary Bowl

The most collectable of all the Victorian salt-glaze wares are the reform cordial flasks which date from the second quarter of the 19th century. These bottles, although they appear to be decorative items, were originally made to hold some sort of liquor, called cordial (an early dictionary describes this as 'liqueur, an alcoholic drink'). The bottles caricature royal and political personalities associated with the Reform Act of 1832; they were really political cartoons of the day. There are eight different flasks in all (Plate 1), each one beautifully moulded and generally regarded by collectors as being superior to flasks produced by other potteries. The personalities portrayed by the flasks are:

1. John Bull seated on a beer barrel
   (impressed XXX SUCCESS TO REFORM)
2. Lord Brougham
   (impressed THE SECOND MAGNA CARTA – BROUGHAM'S REFORM CORDIAL)
3. Lord Grey
   (impressed THE PEOPLES RIGHTS – GREYS REFORM CORDIAL)
4. Queen Victoria
   (impressed VICTORIA – MAY PEACE AND PROSPERITY PREVAIL – QUEEN ALEXANDRINA VICTORIA)
5. Lord John Russell
   (impressed THE TRUE SPIRIT OF REFORM – LORD JOHN RUSSELL)
6. Daniel O'Connell
   (impressed IRISH REFORM CORDIAL – DANIEL O'CONNELL ESQ)
7. William IV
   (impressed WILLIAM IV'S REFORM CORDIAL)
8. Peace, holding a dove (Queen Adelaide)

Each flask is clearly marked on the reverse side with either one of two different impressed marks (see marks A and B in the glossary of marks later in the book):

BOURNES POTTERIES DENBY & CODNOR PARK (flasks 1, 4, 6 and 8)
BOURNES POTTERIES BELPER & DENBY DERBYSHIRE (flasks 2, 3, 5 and 7)

It is impossible to date the marks accurately, but it is logical that the Belper & Denby mark is the earlier, as the Bournes owned both the potteries at Belper and Denby from 1812 to 1834 (when Belper Pottery was closed); in 1833, the Codnor Park Works (owned by W A Burton) was taken over by the Bournes, and was owned by them until its closure in 1861.

There is one flask referred to in Derek Askey's book *Stoneware Bottles* which has no pottery mark; the flask is a flattened ovoid shape and has Victoria's head in an oval plaque on the front, and the Duchess of Kent similarly displayed on the reverse. We are certain that this was originally produced by the Joseph Bourne factory, as copies were made from the original moulds in the 1960s at Denby (Figure 4).

The inexperienced collector should be cautious when purchasing Denby reform cordial flasks as most of the range was reproduced in the 1960s. These were made by Denby Pottery primarily for the American market, and were re-created using the original moulds but using glaze which simulated salt-glazing. Of the eight flasks described above the only two which were not reproduced were Lord Grey and Peace. The reproduction flasks are becoming collectors' items in their own right, although the finest examples are relatively hard to find as most were exported. Many of the pieces bear the later Bourne Denby oval mark

PLATE 1. *Salt-glazed reform flasks, 1830s*

PLATE 2. *Salt-glazed money box, circa 1840, and salt-glazed loving cup with cherubs playing musical instruments, circa 1825–30*

PLATE 3. *Collection of miscellaneous 19th century salt-glazed bottles and jars*

PLATE 4. *Selection of Denby Colours pieces from the late 19th/early 20th century, all with greyhound handles*

PLATE 5. *Ginger beer bottles with a variety of glazes and closures*

(see mark DD in the glossary of marks later in the book), with the words 'Made in England', or the 'scroll' mark with the words 'Antique Reproduction'. Other reproductions of earlier salt-glazed items produced by the factory in the 1960s and early 1970s included Pistol spirit flask, Toby jug, Puzzle jug, Victorian vase, Daisy jug, Monkey jug and various Hunting mugs and jugs.

Other decorative salt-glazed ware of the Victorian period is invariably unmarked and is difficult to identify to all except the experienced salt-glaze collector. The process of throwing salt into the kiln produced a marvellous shiny glaze, but colour and shading varies greatly according to the position of the individual items within the beehive kilns.

Early Denby salt-glaze often has a creamy-yellow colour tinged with honey; they also produced brown salt-glazed decorative wares (often referred to as a 'Nottingham' glaze). If the ware is sprigged it is more easily recognisable. The two main features are the wind-

Figure 4. Reproduction flask, circa 1960, with moulded portrait of Queen Victoria

mill, with a cornfield dipping to the left, and either a willow-type tree or, more commonly, an oak tree (Figures 5, 7 and 8).

On jugs and handled bowls, there is invariably a greyhound handle (Figure 9), which is another means of identification that the piece may be from the Denby factory (although this feature is commonly found on pottery made in the Brampton area of Chesterfield too). Also on jugs, if there is a plain handle, then the design on the strapping at the point where the handle is joined on the base of the jug is yet another means of identification (Figure 10).

Decorative salt-glazed pieces from the Bourne factory are quite rare these days and usually command high prices if in good condition. There is a wide variety in the nature and range of the pieces – loving cups, inkwells, tobacco jars, tygs (three-handled mugs), hunting mugs and jugs, shaving mugs, drug jars, and so on. Some of these items are personalised, often bearing name, date and sometimes a village or town name incised into the body of the pot.

A very rare type of 19th-century salt-glazed Denby is the combination of a brown lustrous 'Nottingham' glaze together with sprigs which are almost black in colour; two such pieces are shown in Figure 12. Some of these can be seen in

*Figure 5. Windmill sprig,
circa 1830–70*

*Figure 7. Oak tree sprig most commonly
used in conjunction with the earlier
windmill (Figure 5)*

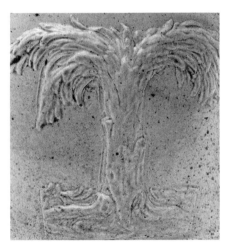

*Figure 8. Willow tree sprig used most
commonly in conjunction with the later
windmill (Figure 6)*

*Figure 6. Windmill sprig (second half of
19th century and early 20th century)*

Figure 9. Greyhound-handled salt-glazed jug (left), with the inscription on the jug shown in detail below

Figure 10. Bunch of grapes and vine leaf used at the base of the handle

Figure 11. Pair of 19th century salt-glazed, barley twist candlesticks

Figure 12.
Large jug and
tobacco jar
displaying more
unusual dark
brown sprigging

the Museum at Denby Pottery and there are other fine examples in the Derby City Museum and Art Gallery.

Sprigged wares with windmills, trees, hunting scenes with dogs, topers (usually a man drinking, sitting astride a barrel) and smokers, were extremely popular during the mid and late Victorian era. The most easily obtainable of Denby sprigged ware is that which the catalogues describe as Denby Colours, that is, a milk chocolate brown glazed top with a putty/oatmeal-coloured bottom half (it is this that is really the Denby Colour as the glaze is a transparent one, thus showing the colour of the Denby clay through the glaze). This glaze and colour combination started to be produced during the second half of the 19th century. The sprigged pottery produced with this glaze is commonly known as 'harvest ware' – the range of items available was initially similar to the salt-glazed wares, for example, hunting mugs, jugs, bowls, tygs, and so on.

Beginning in the 1870s and 1880s, a wider variety of items was available including puzzle jugs, game dishes, beakers, druggists shop pots and snuff jars, tobacco jars (which usually had an unglazed presser inside), teapots, cruet items,

Figure 13.
Group of three
druggists jars
(the two on the
left are salt-
glazed, the one
on the right is
in Denby
Colours)

Figure 14. Water filter, circa 1900

even water filters. Very few, if any, of these wares bear a Denby mark; there is often an impressed capital letter on the unglazed base – this is the thrower's mark and/or, in the case of jugs, the figureman. There is often also an impressed star mark too.

Close examination of the windmill sprigs on various pots will reveal that there are two different ones. The one described earlier as having a cornfield dipping to the left (Figure 5) is quoted by Oswald, Hildyard and Hughes in *English Brown Stoneware (1670-1900)* as being used during the second quarter of the 19th century; the taller windmill with larger sails, and with three windows and a door, was certainly used into the 20th century (Figure 6). It is not at all clear as to the date of the cessation of the one and the introduction of the other. In our research, we have seen dated pieces with the earlier windmill into the 1870s, and the earliest dated piece with the later windmill appears on a beaker with a silver rim, which is hall-marked 1879.

Finally, there is evidence to suggest that the Pottery at Denby was commissioned to produce sprigged tygs, loving cups, beakers and jugs for universities, colleges and special occasions, which included sporting events, masonic functions, and presentations (Figures 15 and 16).

Figure 15. Tennis jug, circa 1900

Figure 16. Tyg with greyhound handles and Oxford University crest

3

Horticultural Wares

IN the advertisements in the *Pottery Gazettes* of the late 19th century, J Bourne and Son publicised their production of Horticultural and Terracotta Wares.

Certainly the pottery started to produce items for the horticultural trade as early as the 1850s. Ceramic plant labels (Figure 17) were originally commissioned by a Professor Daubeny for a Pinetum planted in the Oxford University Parks between 1850 and 1860. Examples of these ceramic plant labels were originally displayed on Joseph Bourne's trade stand at the Great Exhibition of 1851; the entry in the Catalogue of the Great Exhibition reads 'Garden labels, faced with white enamel and lettered in black which, from their impervious nature, are well-adapted for arboretums, pleasure grounds &c.' Although these items are rarely offered for sale today at auctions or antique fairs or shops, a few can still be seen *in situ* in ornamental parks and gardens; there are some good examples to be seen too, in the Museum at Denby Pottery.

The ceramic labels (often called tallies) are in unglazed stoneware with a raised 'scroll' on the face side bearing the name J Bourne; the horticultural name of the plant, tree or shrub is in black, hand-painted lettering which is coated with slip

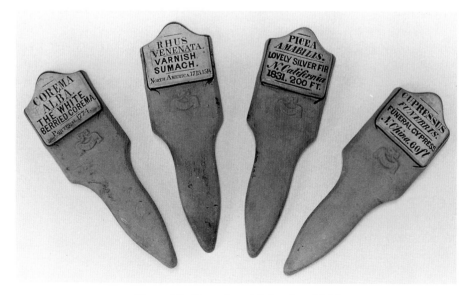

Figure 17. Four plant labels, circa 1851

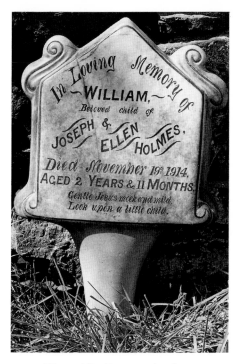

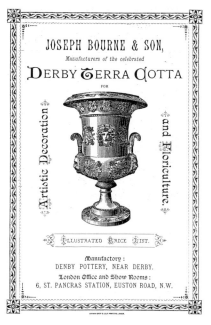

Figure 18. Cemetery headstone

Figure 19. Cover of illustrated price list for 'Artistic Decoration and Horticulture'

and a transparent glaze. There is evidence which suggests that the Denby factory also produced small, simple headstones (which often marked infant and child graves) (Figure 18), and these bear a striking resemblance to the ceramic plant labels.

Also produced were ornamental vases (18 inches high) and large garden vases (20 inches high); these were in a brown salt-glaze and had applied fruit and leaf decorations (Figure 19). Referring once again to the Catalogue of the Great Exhibition (1851), the section on J Bourne, Denby reads 'Specimens of articles made from the same stoneware clay, in the "biscuit" or unglazed state, as garden urns, flower pots, scents jars &c.' No documentary evidence exists on the range or extent of other horticultural products produced, apart from the price list shown in Figure 19.

4

Bottles

TURNING to the more utilitarian ware of the Victorian and Edwardian eras, bottles of many different types were made in profusion: the throwers in the 19th century produced well over 1,000 bottles per man, per 12-hour shift, and the 1908 catalogue proudly states that 'Joseph Bourne and Son's Ginger Beer Bottles have the reputation of a century for their non-absorbent quality, strength and durability. They were made in every known variety of glaze . . .'

The Catalogue of the 1851 Great Exhibition says of Joseph Bourne, Denby Pottery, Derby, 'This manufacturer has the merit of making stoneware bottles which have the property of resisting the action of blacking in a manner which had been found extremely difficult of attainment. Their bottles are consequently employed to a large extent by Messrs. Day and Martin in the export trade to India and elsewhere. The Jury have awarded Mr. Bourne a Prize Medal!'

The Pottery at Denby was probably the leading bottle producer in the whole country for several decades. Bottles were made in every conceivable shape and size for the retailing of inks (with and without spouts), ale, porter and ginger beer, polish (blacking, harness brass and varnish), and handled flagons (up to as large as 24 quarts!). Jars were made for preserves, pickles, extracts, marmalade, honey, fruit, jelly and for storage.

Figure 20. Two salt-glazed ink bottles with original labels, circa 1900

Most of the ginger beer bottles and flagons bear an impressed Denby mark, which is usually on the side of the pot near to the base. There are five basic marks to be found on bottles (see the illustrations and details given under pottery marks C, D, E, F and M in the glossary of marks later in the book), and the latter mark (mark M) is mainly to be found on ginger beer bottles. There are, however, several variations on this oval mark:

(a) just with the words Bourne Denby and no other impressed mark within the oval;

(b) as (a), but with a number in the centre of the oval mark which denotes the year of manufacture – the earliest known date of this mark is 1898, the latest is 1949;

(c) as (a), but with a short horizontal dash in the centre of the oval;

(d) with the name Bourne Denby, but with an impressed letter in the centre – A, B, C or D (no one really knows which dates these indicate; were they pre-1898 or were they produced during World War I?);

(e) with the name Bourne Eastwood (this was a small pottery which Denby acquired around 1900) (see mark N in the glossary of marks later in the book).

There are, however, variations of the other marks, and it is possible to find other impressed marks on bottles – the mark shown in Figure 21 (mark G) is quite a rare one and probably dates from the 1890s.

There were three basic glaze types in ginger beer bottles:

1. Brown salt-glaze
2. Denby Colours, that is a chocolate brown top, with a buff-coloured bottom half
3. A whitish dip-glaze.

Many bottles had the name, town and trade mark underglazed on the side of

Figure 21. Two miniature bottles (0.8 inch high) in front of the rare Bourne impressed mark on a full-size ginger beer bottle

the bottle (see the chapter on 'Advertising Wares' for further details).

Salt-glazed ginger beer bottles were still made into the 1920s; the old ovens were dispensed with in 1931. Ginger beer bottles continued to be made through until 1949, when stoneware bottles finally gave way to their glass counterparts.

The shape of ginger beer bottles tends to vary with the closure patents – cork closure, internal screw stopper, swing stopper and crown cork closure, the latter of which is still used today (Figure 22). Very small miniatures (0.8 inch high) were made as traveller's samples (see Figure 21) – these are very rare, particularly if they are underglazed or impressed with the name Bourne, Denby.

Figure 22. Types of ginger beer bottles: champagne shape, cork or screw mouth (left); with porcelain swing stopper (centre); with top to take crown cork (right)

5

Commemorative, Presentational and Personalised Wares

THE Denby factory has never made commemorative wares as a large-scale enterprise, but it has, nevertheless, over the years produced a wide range of pottery to celebrate special royal, national and even local occasions. The most renowned and well-photographed piece is the Wesley Centenary Bowl which is dated 1839 (see Figure 3). It is not certain whether this is a 'one-off' commissioned piece or whether it is the last remaining example of a limited edition. However, this bowl is typical of the fine quality of salt-glazed pottery produced in Derbyshire during the 19th century.

Personalised and dated pieces made by Joseph Bourne at this time are both rare and valuable. Although many of the outstanding pieces are now in museums and private collections, it is still possible to 'discover' named and dated pieces. Some known examples are:

1. Brown salt-glazed bottle, inscribed George Calton, Denby, May 26th 1813.
2. Small brown salt-glazed inkwell – David Calladine Dec. 25th 1820.
3. Butter churn – Hannah Outram, Knowtshall, Butterley Park, 1835.

Figure 23. Small salt-glazed inkwell dated December 25th 1820

Figure 24. Butter churn inscribed Hannah Outram, Knowtshall, Butterley Park, 1835

Figure 26. Salt-glazed inkwell (Willm Hunt, Riddings, 1857), with reverse side shown below

Figure 25. Salt-glazed shaving mug (George Todd, 1857)

4. Greyhound-handled, sprigged jug, impressed W.DALE PILESLEY 1839.
5. Shaving mug with 'tree' handle, impressed GEORGE TODD 1857.
6. Brown salt-glazed inkwell with relief-moulded sprigs of Royal Coat-of-Arms, monkey smoking pipe, and windmill; impressed WILL^M HUNT, RIDDINGS, NOV'R 26th 1857.
7. Giant salt-glazed loving cup, with relief-moulded sprigs and impressed names – PRINCE ALBERT, QUEEN VICTORIA & DUCHESS OF KENT; also cornucopia and figures of five men playing brass instruments and impressed JULIENS BAND. The piece is named and dated – JOHN FALL Nov 16th 1858.
8. Puzzle jug, impressed JOHN RILEY 1877.
9. Inkwell, in Denby Colours, underglazed W. Clarke October 1st. 1878.
10. Money box, impressed L. BATES.
11. Presentation jug with 'harvest-ware' sprigs and EPNS top, made in 1880 as a rowing trophy for the 'Trial Eights' for KRC (Kingston Rowing Club?); the names of the eight crew and the cox are inscribed on a shield attached to the metal rim.
12. Harvest Ware tyg in Denby Colours, with greyhound handles and silver rim engraved 'Hertford College Scratch Fours 1888'.
13. Jug with trefoil top, 'Manufactured to commemorate the Signal Conservative Success in July 1895 – Giles Greene McCalmont – Cambridgeshire

Figure 27. Giant salt-glazed loving cup, named and dated John Fall, Nov 16th 1858

Figure 29. Jug with trefoil top commemorating a Conservative election success in 1895

Figure 30. (Above) Loving cup with greyhound handles and inscription John Wiln, Cromford, 1896. (Below) The frog inside the base

Figure 28. Brown salt-glazed jug commemorating KRC 'Trial Eights' 1880

– Jebb Gorst Penrose-Fitzgerald'. It also bears a shield with the Latin inscription 'Magna est veritas et Praevalebit'.

14. Loving cup with frog inside, in Denby Colours and having greyhound handles – sgraffito inscription John Wiln, Cromford, 1896.
15. Jug made in honour of the Relief of Mafeking, dated 1900.
16. Loving cup, made to commemorate the end of the 19th century ('Fin de Siècle'), and also the sixty-fourth year of Queen Victoria's reign.
17. Loving cup with greyhound handles and frog inside – underglazed Thomas Fenn 1898
18. Loving cup, again with frog and greyhound handles – underglazed D. Storer 1904.
19. Footed loving cup in Denby Colours with relief-moulded sprigs and greyhound handles – inscribed A memento of Mr. Nickall's visit to Denby Pottery 23.8.12.

Examples 15 and 16 are described in more detail in the chapter on 'Arts and Crafts Decorative Pottery'.

Many of the personalised and presentation pieces made by the Pottery just before and after the turn of the century have incised inscriptions, usually in cobalt blue. This was probably due to the influence of the entrepreneur, Horace Elliott, who had some of his designs produced at Denby around this time (for further details, see 'Arts and Crafts Decorative Pottery'). Many of the pieces described above, made in the 1890s and early 1900s, have this style of inscription. Another such example, undated, is shown in Figure 31; the inscription is part of the chorus of a well-known song:

> Glorious Beer!
> Up with the sale of it
> Down with a pail of it
> Glorious, Glorious Beer!

On the base of this beaker is the name of the retailer, Albert W Boak, 19 Town Hill, Wrexham.

Figure 31. Beaker with inscribed rhyme
'Glorious Beer!'

Royal Events

Excluding the reform cordial flasks which have already been described in chapter 2, the earliest known royal commemorative from the Joseph Bourne factory dates from 1840 when relief moulded salt-glazed mugs and jugs were made to celebrate the marriage of Queen Victoria to Prince Albert. Also produced around this time was a flask with raised head and shoulder portraits – on the front, in an oval with a raised head, is Queen Victoria, and on the rear in similar guise is the Duchess of Kent (Victoria's mother) (see the chapter on 'Nineteenth-Century Wares', including Figure 4).

Figure 32. Small salt-glazed mustard pot commemorating Queen Victoria's marriage in 1840

Although Joseph Bourne exhibited at the Great Exhibition of 1851, there is no evidence to show that any special commemorative items were made to celebrate this memorable occasion. We have to wait until 1887 for Victoria's Golden Jubilee for the next commemorative pieces to be produced; these again take the form of mugs and jugs, either with a relief moulded head and shoulders within an oval frame (with the dates 1837 and 1887 set in rectangular slabs on either side), or, more ornately, some exhibited royal coat of arms in addition to flags and flowers, and a crown at the base of the handle; most of these were made in Denby Colours, that is, buff-coloured base with a milk-chocolate coloured top.

The 1897 Diamond Jubilee saw yet another range of mugs and jugs with the same moulding used for the plaque of Queen Victoria, but this time the dates were more prominent with more ornate numbers set in swags; the tops of many of these appear in a dark green glaze instead of the usual chocolate brown. Some of the smaller 1897 Jubilee Mugs have an underglazed monochrome transfer of Victoria's head and dates, above which is the inscription 'She wrought her People Lasting Good' and beneath is 'Sixty Years Progress'. This former inscription is also to be found on a rare large jug with trefoil

Figure 33. Victoria Diamond Jubilee decorative jug with trefoil top and fine, detailed sprigs and bearing inscription 'She wrought her People Lasting Good'

top, and the highly decorated letters VR together with crown, date and sprays consisting of an English rose, Scottish thistle and Irish shamrock.

Another interesting and unusual Victoria commemorative is the beaker (Figure 34) which has three underglazed medallions of Victoria as a young woman on her accession to the throne in 1837, as she appeared at her Golden Jubilee in 1887, and as an old lady at her Diamond Jubilee in 1897. The text beneath reads 'The Pillar of a People's Hope, The Centre of a World's Desire'. These beakers were almost certainly commissioned for Cambridge University, as on the reverse side, in sgraffito, blue lettering is 'Floreat Cantabridgia'.

Mugs and beakers were produced to commemorate the 1902 Coronation of Edward VII and the 1911 Coronation of George V; the design of these is identical, with the heads of the King and Queen on opposite sides and in between a banner with the words 'Coronation of . . .' and the appropriate date. It is interesting to note that most of the mugs produced for the 1911 Coronation have a lavender-blue

Figure 34. Victoria Diamond Jubilee beaker (1897) with motto 'The Pillar of a People's Hope, The Centre of a World's Desire'

top instead of the usual chocolate brown or dark green.

Some of the Denby commemorative wares of the Victorian and Edwardian eras do not bear the Denby impressed mark; they often bear the mark of Mortlock's Ltd, Oxford Street, London W, who was the country's leading retailer of commemorative wares around this time. As much of the commemorative ware produced by Joseph Bourne was sold in the Denby and Ripley locality, many of the pieces have the Derbyshire village impressed or underglazed on to the pottery, for example Ripley,

Figure 35. Mortlock's Ltd mark often found on the base of late Victorian and Edwardian commemorative pieces

PLATE 6. *Victorian Commemorative Ware*
(Golden and Diamond Jubilees, 1887 and 1897)

PLATE 7. *1902 and 1911 Coronation Mugs with local place names*
(from left to right: Ripley, Waingroves and Lower Kilbourne)

PLATE 8. *Collection of Danesby Majolica Ware, circa 1900*

PLATE 9. *Majolica teapot – Mrs A Ramsden 1902*

PLATE 10. *Majolica epergne with lustres*

PLATE 11. *Large 'classical shaped' Majolica vase*

Figure 36. 1930s Royal Commemoratives
From left to right: Edward VIII Coronation (1937); King George V/Queen Mary
Silver Jubilee (1935); Coronation of King George VI (1937)

Waingroves, Marehay, Breadsall, and even Denby itself. Rarer inscriptions include Heage, Kilburn (usually spelt in the old form of Kilbourne) and Denby Bottles and Rousen Green (now known locally as Rawson Green).

Commemorative mugs were also made for the George V Silver Jubilee in 1935, and the Coronation of George VI in 1937; they were even made for the Coronation of Edward VIII but these are quite rare. The design for all of these three mugs is the same; a relatively unattractive one, having a rather rounded, barrel shape with an Epic Green glaze and a basic decoration.

The 1953 Coronation of Queen Elizabeth II saw several shapes of mug produced:

1. Basic straight-sided, cream-glazed with transfer coat-of-arms decoration; many of those in circulation were presented to the schoolchildren in mid-Derbyshire.
2. Larger and footed, with a more bell-shaped top and having a grey glaze.
3. Straight-sided in a green, brown or dark blue glaze having a gold band top and bottom.
4. A two-handled loving cup, usually in green glaze.

There were, however, several variants of these four main shapes; also produced was a large 2-pint bulbous-shaped jug in either blue, brown or green glaze, with the Coronation emblem blazoned on it.

In more recent times, mugs (using

Figure 37. Coronation mug 1953

Figure 38. Group of Queen Elizabeth Coronation (1953) commemorative pieces

Denby's then-current production-line shapes), loving cups and beakers were produced to mark the Queen's Silver Jubilee in 1977 and the marriage of Prince Charles to Lady Diana Spencer in 1981. Two different designs of plates were also made to commemorate the latter occasion. No other royal commemoratives, however, have been produced since this date.

Figure 39. 1977 Silver Jubilee mug

Figure 40. Group of Royal Wedding commemoratives (1981)

Other Commemorative Wares

As mentioned previously, the Denby Pottery did not produce any items to commemorate the Great Exhibition of 1851, nor did they make any special pottery for their centenary in 1909 – all employees were presented with a medal with a picture of the Pottery on one side and Mr and Mrs Bourne-Wheeler on the reverse.

Figure 41. 1909 Denby Pottery Centenary medal

The following list, which is far from comprehensive, represents a very small proportion of the many hundreds of commemorative pottery mugs and other items that have been produced by the factory in the 20th century:

1. Commemorative mug for the visit of 'Their Majesties' to Shirebrook on June 25, 1914.
2. Peace celebration mug, marking the end of The Great War in 1919. These mugs have an underglazed picture of Britannia holding the dove and usually have the name of a particular village or town under this.
3. Mug made as 'A Memento of the Golden Wedding of William & Lady Nora FitzHerbert, October 24th 1949'.

Figure 42. Two 1919 Peace Celebration mugs with underglazed village names

4. Tankard made to commemorate the 150th anniversary of the Denby Pottery (1809-1959).
5. Mug made for the centenary of the Goodspeed Opera House in East Haddam, Connecticut, in 1976.
6. Mug for the Eyam (Derbyshire) School Centenary in 1977.
7. Mug made for the Bob Taylor Testimonial Reception at Chatsworth in 1981, which highlights his world record wicketkeeping 1,371 catches in

Figure 44. Group of more modern commemoratives/advertising mugs

Figure 45. Two modern commemorative plates: last firing at Langley Mill Pottery 1982 (left); Langley Collector's Society, 1992 (right)

first-class cricket 1960–1981, and his world record dismissals in a test match – India *v.* England, Bombay, March 1980.

8. Plate especially commissioned to commemorate the final firing at the Langley Pottery in December 1982.

9. Mug produced for Ross Catherall Ceramics to celebrate their twentieth anniversary in 1989.

10. Plate (limited edition) made to commemorate the founding of the Langley Collectors' Society in March 1992.

The story, however, does not end here, as it is still possible today for visitors to the factory to have individual pieces made and hand-decorated in celebration of birthdays, anniversaries, christenings and other special occasions.

6

Majolica

THE name and the origins are somewhat elusive for this range of pottery, first introduced in early 1886 and finally discontinued circa 1935. It is not true Majolica as this was the name that the Minton factory gave to brightly-coloured

wares similar to the tin-glazed Italian earthenwares. The documentary evidence about the design and available shapes is rather fragmentary. Its striking appearance is typified by its random royal blue and tan mottled, shiny glaze.

The only catalogue evidence that we can trace dates from Edwardian times (around 1908) and illustrates only ten different shapes of 'Danesby Flower Vases'.

It is certainly interesting to note that, although an article in the *Pottery Gazette* of March 1886 refers to the new Danesby Ware (a title which was more commonly used in connection with the art wares produced in the 1930s), only a handful of pieces bear the impressed mark on the unglazed bases (see mark L in the glossary of marks later in the book).

Evidence from our twenty years research into 'antique Denby' would seem to suggest that the first Majolica vases and other decorative items were potted very much in the Victorian style – large ewers with massive curved, flamboyant handles, table-centre epergnes with glass lustres, decorative shoes, two-tier money boxes with elaborate finials. The page of the

Figure 46. Shapes from the Majolica Catalogue, circa 1908

catalogue shown in Figure 46 possibly dates from 1908 and includes the 'cooling tower' flower tubes which were widely produced by several different Derbyshire stoneware potteries between 1900 and 1915.

Another interesting discovery, is that Denby Majolica also appears in a much rarer green form which we can be certain, from our research, was mainly produced in the 1890s.

Production of the Majolica glaze certainly continued into the mid-1930s (pig money boxes are known to bear a date of 1935, also tobacco jars continued to be made for smoker's cabinets). It is, however, almost certain that large-scale production of general Majolica wares, such as vases and bowls, ceased in the mid-1920s, when the J Bourne & Son's factory turned their attention towards more decorative and colourful tube-lined wares.

Over the years several interesting 'finds' in Denby Majolica have emerged, but by far the most unusual is an inkwell in the shape of a boot. This was a design called 'Triumph' which was patented by James Marshall of Fulham around 1906. The patent incorporated a screw which could be turned to control the level of ink in the inkwell, and the grooves in the screw-top acted as a pen rest. The Doulton, Lambeth, pottery also developed this patent inkwell and produced decorated versions of it.

Figure 47. 'Triumph' boot inkwell, circa 1906, with the impressed mark on the base shown above

7

Arts and Crafts Decorative Pottery

A RTS AND CRAFTS pieces are rarities, and there are several examples to be seen in the Museum at Denby. They are easily recognisable with their grey or buff-coloured glaze with incised decorations and inscriptions in blue (sgraffito). The two most notable designers/potters who created pieces in the style of this movement were Horace Elliott and J C Wheeler.

Horace Elliott

Many pieces are found to be unmarked; some, however, have the impressed mark Elliott, London, and a fleur-de-lys mark. Horace Elliott was a London designer, decorator, and dealer in art pottery and made regular visits to Ewenny Pottery in South Wales between 1883 and 1913; some of his work from this pottery is listed in the catalogues of the Arts and Crafts Exhibition Society. He was an entrepreneur and had a pottery shop in Chelsea and later in Streatham Hill. What is certain is that he had some striking decorative pieces made to his designs at the Bourne factory at Denby circa 1900. Known pieces include:

1. Stoneware loving cup made to commemorate the 'Fin de Siècle', and each of the four handles is in the shape of the figures of the date 1900. The inscriptions incised into the cup are:

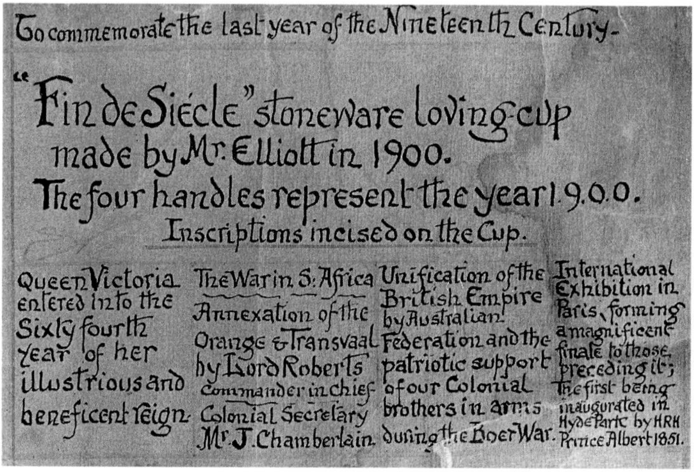

Figure 48. Text (from the original parchment) of the incised inscriptions on the 'Fin de Siècle' loving cup

To commemorate the last year of the Nineteenth Century.

"Fin de Siècle" stoneware loving-cup made by Mr. Elliott in 1900.
The four handles represent the year 1.9.0.0.
Inscriptions incised on the Cup.

Queen Victoria entered into the Sixty fourth year of her illustrious and beneficent reign.

The War in S. Africa — Annexation of the Orange & Transvaal by Lord Roberts Commander in chief Colonial Secretary Mr. J. Chamberlain.

Unification of the British Empire by Australian Federation and the patriotic support of our Colonial brothers in arms during the Boer War.

International Exhibition in Paris, forming a magnificent finale to those preceding it; The first being inaugurated in Hyde Park by HRH Prince Albert 1851.

'Queen Victoria entered into the sixty fourth year of her illustrious and beneficial reign'

'The War in S. Africa – Annexation of the Orange and Transvaal by Lord Roberts, Commander in Chief Colonial Secretary Mr. J. Chamberlain'

'Unification of the British Empire by Australian Federation and the patriotic support of our Colonial brothers in arms during the Boer War'

'International Exhibition in Paris forming a magnificent finale to those preceding it, the first being inaugurated in Hyde Park by HRH Prince Albert 1851'.

2. Ornamental candlestick bearing the Biblical inscription 'Neither do men light a candle and put it under a bushel, but on a candlestick and it giveth light to all that are in the house S.Matt.5:15'.

3. Pig money box – 'This pig went to market'.

4. Jug with decorative handle – 'This jug was made and inscribed during the week after Colonel Mahon's relief column marched into Mafeking and the handle I designed and fixed in honour of this unique event in England's history. Horace Elliott'.

5. Decorative bowl – 'This bowl was made on the day that Ladysmith was relieved by General Sir Redvers Butler, March 1st. 1900, after 4 months siege.'

6. Wine server, having the underglazed inscription 'May 1st – the twenty fifth anniversary of the day on which James Parkin began to work at Denby Pottery'.

7. Decorative coffee pot, with a rather macabre inscription – 'In affectionate memory of Harry Godkin who was working on this jug as an apprentice at Denby Pottery when seized with the sickness which ended his life, on Monday afternoon February 2nd. 1903'.

8. Pig money box, inscribed to Nellie Wagstaff with the motto 'Never waste the muckles and the muckles then you'll keep'.

9. Salt-glazed jug with greyhound handle –

> 'Few handcraft can with our trade compare
> We make our wares of what we potters are = clay',

and on the reverse side

> 'Some won't drink this, some won't drink that and some have
>   notions queer;
> But to my mind 'tis hard to find a drink as good as beer'.

Figure 49. Ornamental candlestick by Elliott with biblical inscribed text

Figure 50. In Memoriam coffee pot by Elliott dated February 2nd 1903

Figure 51. Salt-glazed jug, circa 1900, with sgraffito text

Figure 52. Small salt-glazed jug with sgraffito hen decoration by J C Wheeler, dated 1895

J C Wheeler

Collectors of art pottery, and in particular pieces by the Martin Brothers and also by Hannah and Florence Barlow at the Doulton factory, will be familiar with sgraffito designs of animals, birds and fish.

Similar wares, which bear some resemblance to these were produced at Denby (circa 1895–1900) by a certain J C A Wheeler, commonly called 'Willie'. He was the brother of Joseph Bourne-Wheeler, who ran the pottery jointly with Mr Topham; he was a minister of religion and ran a boys' preparatory school. His potting was done in his school holidays when he visited Denby Pottery. Pieces by him usually bear the incised initials JCW or JCAW on the base and are often dated.

Most of the known pieces by J C Wheeler are jugs or vases with cobalt blue sgraffito geese, ducks and birds, plus associated flora such as reeds and bulrushes. The overall glaze is usually a transparent one, that is, Denby Colours. There is one known piece – a small jug – by J C Wheeler which again has sgraffito decoration, but the finish is one of brown salt-glaze.

8

General Domestic and Utilitarian Wares

DOMESTIC stoneware over the years, must account for at least 75 per cent of Denby's total production. The early 20th-century catalogues describe this as 'General Stoneware'. Nowadays, these collectables come under the heading of 'Kitchenalia' and this title covers a multitude of bottles, jars, jugs and basins connected with cooking, baking, storing and preserving.

In the Victorian and Edwardian eras, before the days of convenience foods, families baked their own bread, made their own jams, pickles and preserves, and cooked a wide range of stews and casseroles, usually on an open fire or in a side oven. There is currently an upsurge in collecting Kitchenalia, and now, old functional domestic items are being used as decorative objects in homes, bars and restaurants. Sadly, one rarely finds good examples of the more unusual items of early Denby domestic stoneware today, as they were merely everyday pieces of pottery which were discarded when they had become outdated or outlived their usefulness.

Stoneware pottery was the most versatile material used to produce numerous utensils for all these domestic tasks, and Joseph Bourne and Son's factory at Denby was the leading manufacturer for many decades. The range was very extensive and included stewpots, bread pans, covered butter jars, souse pots, mixing bowls, colanders, baking dishes, pipkins, churns, mortars and pestles, jelly moulds,

Figure 53. Group of 19th-century salt-glazed jars, pots and electrical insulators

barrels, storage jars, water filters, jugs and pitchers, tobacco pots, spittoons, bird feeders, and so on – the list is seemingly endless.

A comprehensive list of cooking, baking and serving wares was still available, up to the 1920s, in the original brown, salt-glazed form. Extremely popular was the range of wares produced in Denby Colours; also, the Denby factory was one of the first to introduce a variety of 'plain' colours, including brown, matt black, ruby and green. The famous Chocolate Ware (dark brown and chocolate colour overall, but with a roughened band around the lower half of the pottery) was first introduced in 1895, and the advertising material of the time proudly boasts 'their splendid heat-retaining qualities are unrivalled for making tea, coffee and cocoa in perfection'. Also popular were the Chef Ware and the British Fireproof Ware.

The printed catalogue extracts provide an interesting cross-section of some of the differing shapes and sizes available. We have, however, chosen to single out some of the more fascinating areas of collecting within this vast array of utensils in the hope that the information, together with the illustrations, will provide collectors with an insight into this increasingly popular field of collectables.

Teapots

For the many collectors of teapots, there is a wide variety of shapes and sizes to provide interest.

Joseph Bourne and Son started to produce teapots in large quantities in the early 20th century. Prior to this, the emphasis was mainly on cookware, as tea and coffee drinking was mainly associated with fine china and silver. Although the Brampton (Chesterfield) potteries produced decorative teapots (Figure 54)

Figure 54. Brampton (Chesterfield) salt-glazed decorative teapot

51

Figure 55. *Shapes illustrated in the catalogue*

and coffee pots which, in shape and style, emulated their silver counterparts, stoneware teaware was not mass produced until the 20th century. Stoneware teapots, coffee pots, milk and cream jugs, and sugar basins offered a cheaper alternative to china and silver, mainly for the working classes.

The 1904 Denby catalogue lists some interestingly named shapes, which were available from capacities of ¼ pint up to 2 quarts (4 pints). Most were available in Denby Colours but there were variants of this, such as with a Roughened Centre or Beaded (with a beaded band between the two colours). Shapes included Gipsy, Silver, Indian and Venetian, and the Gipsy could also be purchased with a metal cover, available in two different qualities (called 'Cheap Mount' and 'Best Mount'). The Gipsy teapot was also available in a one-cup size, along with a miniature cream jug and sugar basin called a 'Four o'clock Tea Set'.

More expensive, and very collectable now, were the figural teapots (which we have earlier called 'Harvest Ware'); these had sprigged decoration of windmill, oak tree, foxhounds, and so on. One of the best and earliest examples of this type of teapot which is personalised and dated (Mrs William Hall, Kilbourne, 1903), was produced in a semi-matt grey glaze with cobalt blue sprigs. Personalised and dated teapots can also be found in Denby Majolica and later (circa 1930) in Electric Blue.

Figure 56. *19th-century figural teapot*

As we proceed through the Edwardian era, so the range of teapot styles and shapes continued to be extended. New ranges of coloured stoneware became available – Brown and Green Ware, and Emerald Ware (green inside and outside) were introduced by 1912, and by 1919 these had been extended to include Celeste Ware (dark blue top half with light blue, rough-textured lower half), Mahogany Ware, and teasets and coffee sets specifically for restaurant use. New shapes of teapot were also introduced – these included the Henley, Varsity, and the Wedgwood! Of particular interest and rarity is the Queen Anne teaset (which was a registered design).

Figure 57. Decorative teapot inscribed to Mrs William Hall, Kilbourne, 1903

Figure 58. Restaurant pattern teapots

New, and revolutionary designs of teapot were produced in the 1920s; the ones which are most interesting to the collector are:

1. The SYP Teapot (meaning Simple Yet Perfect) – this was a most unusual

Figure 59. Queen Anne teaset illustrated in the catalogue

53

THE PATENT "S.Y.P."
TEA POT

SUPPLIED BY ARRANGEMENT WITH THE
PATENTEE

K 104 **Mahogany** ⎱ ½ pt. ¾ pt. pt. 1½ pt. qt.
J 104 **Green** ⎰ **2/9 3/- 3/6 4/- 4/6** each

Figure 60. Catalogue illustration for the SYP teapot

patent that enabled tea to be made in such a way that, when the pot was turned through 90 degrees, the user was able to pour out the tea so leaving the tea leaves in the lid! These patented teapots were not solely made by the Denby company.

2. The 'Nevva Drip' – this was patented with a revolutionary spout. Mrs Gordon-Stables commented in *The Girl's Own Paper and Woman's Magazine* in August 1922 that 'the Nevva-Drip does not accumulate tea leaves in its spout in the reprehensible manner common to many pots, but pours out its brew with commendable straightforwardness'. The 'Nevva-Drip' design has also proved effective for modern-day living, as it was re-introduced by the Denby Pottery Company in 1992.

3. The 'Pekoe' – this was a most intriguing design, having a cube-like shape with flattened handle, stunted spout and recessed lid. It was very much in the Art Deco mode and was, according to the catalogue, 'designed to reduce risk of breakage to handle, spout and lid'.

Figure 61.
Styles available
of 'Nevva-
Drip' teapots

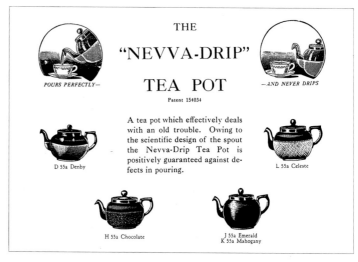

THE

POURS PERFECTLY—

"NEVVA-DRIP"
TEA POT

—AND NEVER DRIPS

Patent 154034

A tea pot which effectively deals with an old trouble. Owing to the scientific design of the spout the Nevva-Drip Tea Pot is positively guaranteed against defects in pouring.

D 55a Denby

L 55a Celeste

H 55a Chocolate

J 55a Emerald
K 55a Mahogany

54

PLATE 12. *Majolica money boxes, circa 1912*

PLATE 13. *Commemorative 'Fin de Siècle' loving cup (1900) by Elliott*

PLATE 14. *Three Elliott commemorative pieces –*
Mafeking jug, decorative bowl and wine server

PLATE 15. *Selection of decorative sgraffito pieces by J C Wheeler*

PLATE 16. *Denby Colours Kitchenalia:*
infusion jug, jelly mould, colander, Gipsy teapot, chocolate pot

PLATE 17. *Selection of salesman's samples for cookware, circa 1920,*
with full-sized ginger beer bottle and coffee pot

PLATE 18. *Three Quaker Brown teapots (the centre one has a 2-gallon capacity)*

PLATE 19. *Four Housekeepers' Jars from different periods*
(from left to right: circa 1912, circa 1925, circa 1935 and circa 1880)

Cottage Blue

Joseph Bourne
& Son, Limited
Denby Pottery, Nr. Derby

London Office & Showroom :
34, HOLBORN VIADUCT, E.C.1

PLATE 20. *Title page from Cottage Blue catalogue*

58

Figure 62. Miniature *'Nevva-Drip'* teapot with patent mark found on underside shown above

Figure 63. Pekoe teapot

Colanders and Jelly Moulds

Denby produced salt-glazed colanders in the 19th century, but it is difficult to identify them as being from the Denby Pottery as they had no impressed mark. More easily recognisable is the colander produced in the Denby Colours – it is possible to find these in antique shops and centres, as well as at collectors' fairs, but it is rare to find the glaze in good condition due to the constant contact with boiling water.

Jelly moulds are always popular and are usually reasonably-priced collectables. Once again, Bourne's Pottery produced them in salt glaze, white glaze and, of course, Denby Colours. The latter types are the most commonly recognisable, and appear in many different shapes and sizes, including one in the form of a rabbit, and a rarer version in the shape of a duck.

DENBY "COTTAGE BLUE" WARE

MOTTLED BLUE OUTSIDE, YELLOW INSIDE

TEA POTS

The "Nevva-Drip" (Patent) 154034

Stuart Shape

Figure 64. Catalogue illustration for Cottage Blue Ware

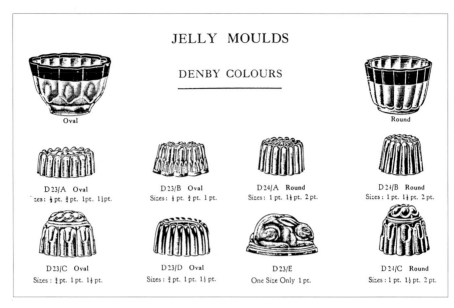

Figure 65. Catalogue illustration for jelly moulds

Storage Jars

These were described in the early catalogues as Housekeeper's Jars; they were produced in a light stone (buff) colour, in varying sizes from ½ pint to 4 quarts, either as a plain, lidded jar, or with a white raised label with the names fired in, for example, sultanas, sugar, oatmeal, loaf sugar, tapioca and so on. When the Cottage Blue first appeared in the mid-1920s, the housekeeper's jars were most attractive as they had tube-lined raised labels.

In the 1930s, the pottery introduced a new series of housekeeper's jars in their 'Denby Kitchen Ware' range. The jars were barrel-shaped, in an off-white, semi-matt glaze with green bands encircling the upper and lower halves and having the label in raised, tube-lined lettering, in-filled with green.

Denby has long been an exporter of stoneware pottery, and housekeeper's jars

Figure 66. Group of Denby Colours jelly moulds

Figure 67.
Catalogue
illustration for
Antique Jugs

were made for export, particularly for France, Germany and Denmark, and naturally the wording for the labels for these appears in the appropriate language.

Housekeeper's jars fell out of fashion after World War II, and it is only in recent years that they have made a comeback in recent Denby ranges with the more up-to-date title of storage jars.

Jugs

Over the years, the Denby Pottery has produced a very varied array of jugs of all shapes and sizes. Aspects of this topic are touched upon in the chapters on 19th century wares, and on advertising wares.

In the last decade of the 19th century, Joseph Bourne and Son produced an interesting range of 'Antique Jugs'. The four shapes that were made (Pompeii, Cambridge, Salisbury and Herculaneum) were all quite elegant-looking jugs, and were based on designs from earlier generations. However, the catalogues of the first thirty years of this century illustrated a bewildering selection of jugs of all shapes and sizes. They could be purchased in a wide range of colours, variations and capacities, and each shape (Figure 68) had its own particular name, for example, Roman, Ship, Tankard, Toby, and Convent! As with other pottery items, they were available in Denby Colours (with greyhound or plain handle), Chocolate Ware, Brown and Green Ware, Emerald and Mahogany Ware, and of course, Cottage Blue and Quaker Brown.

Salt-glazed jugs (having a dark brown top and lighter brown lower half) were

Figure 68.
Catalogue
illustration for
Plain Jugs

made especially for the GPO, and this was usually indicated on the base. They were made either for the pouring of ink, or for pouring water on to the sponge pads.

Jugs could also be purchased with metal covers; they were available in several different mounts – Best, Toft's and Cheap. Jugs were also made in very small sizes; smaller than the ¼ pint were the cream and toy sizes. However, tiny miniatures were also made (not in any great quantities); it is suggested that many of these (often less than 1 inch high), were actually turned on a wheel as something of a competition between the potters.

General Cookware

British Fireproof Ware and Denby Chef Ware were introduced during the first decade of the 20th century. These were produced either in brown or green glazes, but at the same time the salt-glazed cookware continued to be made, but was apparently, by now, less fashionable.

To collectors of Kitchenalia there is a very varied assortment of stewpots, casseroles, entrée dishes and serving dishes which had the advantage (as they still do today) of being oven to tableware. Again, as with the other items of general stoneware already described, they were made in a variety of sizes – the upright shape stewpots and stew jars were made as large as 12 pint capacity (and in 1912, the cost, wholesale, was 66/- [£3.30] per dozen!).

Some of the casseroles and covered saucepans were quite attractive pieces of

Figure 69. GPO jug (top), and jug with Best Mount metal cover (bottom)

Figure 70. Group of Quaker Brown kitchen ware, circa 1930

Figure 71.
Group of
Emerald Green
domestic items

pottery, having rather elegant handles, knobs and finials. A particularly interesting shape in the Chef Ware is the Marmite pot, which either had a brown glaze inside with an unglazed outside or a red (not brown) glaze both inside and out.

These were made in nine different sizes from 12 pints all the way down to ¼ pint (individual).

Denby actually made stoneware utensils for almost every kitchen task imaginable. We have already described colanders and jelly moulds, but the catalogues listed cake pans, baking dishes (both round and square), hot pots (with or without the label), mixing bowls, butter jars and coolers, water coolers (which were unglazed and porous), egg poachers, milk boilers, coffee filters, eared dishes, porridge bowls (a lidded casserole-type pot for the making of porridge), oval dishes for fish, bread storage crocks, soufflé dishes, ramekins, infusion jugs and a quail case!

Very popular with some collectors are lemon squeezers and toast racks. These too, were made

Stewpot

Oval casserole

Covered pipkin

Breakfast entrée dish

Coffee filter

Stew jar

Hot water dish

Marmite

Round casserole
(handled)

Soft cheese dish

*Figure 72. Catalogue illustrations
of general kitchen ware*

in stoneware; the former was available in a green glaze and the latter was made in either a green or a brown glaze, with either three bars or five bars.

Game pie dishes first appeared in the catalogues in the latter part of the 19th century. They were made by many of the leading potteries such as Wedgwood, and were originally produced when flour, for the making of pastry, was in short supply. They were attractive table items, and Denby's version of the game pie dish was available, complete with stoneware lining, either unglazed, that is, in a biscuit finish, or glazed in Denby Colours. The applied relief sprigs were of foliage and pheasants, and the finial on the lid was a model of a hare.

Puzzle jugs were first made in the first half of the 19th century in salt-glaze; these are now very rare indeed and are also very difficult to identify as being produced by the Joseph Bourne factory. The one illustrated in Figure 73 can be

Figure 73. Puzzle jug, inscribed John Riley, 1877

seen in the Denby Museum, but it was produced in the last quarter of the 19th century (it is actually dated 1877). The most easily obtainable were produced in Denby Colours in the first decade of the 20th century, and they feature the conventional 'harvest-ware' sprigging of windmill, tree, toper, and so on.

Both puzzle jugs and game dishes were reproduced in imitation salt-glaze in the late 1960s and early 1970s.

Figure 74. Denby kitchen ware, 1930s

Miscellaneous Functional Items

The rather haunting face jug in Figure 75, often misconstrued as Wellington, is in fact 'Ally Sloper'.

This type of jug was made at Denby towards the end of the 19th century, and appears in both Denby Colours and the salt-glazed version in the illustration. Ally Sloper was the first British comic strip hero, called Alexander Sloper FOM (Friend of Man). His name is really a 'pun on the Victorian poor man's dodge of sloping off down an ally when the rent man came into sight.' Sloper first appeared in the pages of a magazine called *Judy* (similar to *Punch*) in 1867. He became particularly popular in the 1870s and 1880s in a series of annual almanacs and again

Figure 75. Ally Sloper jug, circa 1900

in the 1920s and late 1940s. The jug shown in Figure 75 has the oval impressed Bourne, Denby, Derby mark (see mark I in the glossary of marks later in the book) and also has the name Ally Sloper inscribed in the base.

Candlesticks, in the first half of this century, were quite important items, particularly when the electricity supply was unreliable, or, in some areas, non-existent. Candlesticks and holders were produced in an assortment of colours,

Figure 76. Catalogue illustrations of toilet sets and candlesticks

with pink being the most popular. As Figure 76 suggests there were many variations, tall, low, flat, goblet and shaded.

Even animals and pets were well-catered for; rabbit troughs and fowl fountains were first made by the pottery in the 19th century either with a brown salt-glazed finish or in Denby Colours. A great variety of dog and cat troughs were also made often with raised black lettering or underglazed lettering. The most sought-after, however, of all these, were produced in the 1920s in assorted colours (blue being the most popular) with raised tube-lined lettering in a contrasting colour.

Figure 77. Fowl fountain

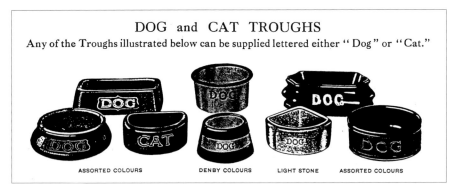

Figure 78. Catalogue illustrations of dog and cat troughs

Certain less salubrious items for everyday use were also made by the factory. Spittoons, which were in common use in public houses earlier this century, were made in salt-glaze, light stone, green, chocolate or Denby Colours; the one produced in the latter glaze had a fluted top and often had applied relief sprigs around the side. Chamber pots or 'potties' too, were important production items and are quite collectable today. It is quite rare to find a Denby one these days;

Figure 79. Catalogue illustrations of spittoons

they were usually made in salt-glaze (with a darker-coloured top), or in Denby Colours.

Toilet sets, consisting of jug and bowl, soap dish, tooth brush holder and beaker, sponge bowl and toilet pail were made by the Pottery, again in a large assortment of colours, including matt black, matt blue, ruby, green, mauve and pink. Dressing table trinket sets were also made in a similar range of colours, the

Figure 80. Electric fire

most popular being pink. These usually consisted of an oval-shaped tray, lidded pots, small oval dishes and ring trees.

Perhaps one of the most unusual pottery items produced by Denby in the 1930s was a stoneware electric fire surround. This was produced in either an Epic Green glaze or in a brown (mahogany) glaze. It is rare to find one of these in this day and age; the one in Denby's own museum is complete with electric element!

9

Hot Water Bottles

HOT water bottles were originally made in salt-glaze in the 19th century. The early catalogues (circa 1860) described them as bed bottles; later, around 1880, they became known as feet bottles, and around the turn of the century they were called footwarmers. It is very interesting to note that the factory sold them to retailers with or without the screw stopper!

The traditional half-moon shaped profile has changed little throughout the 100 or more years that they have been made; but there have been many other shapes created during that time, for both functional and decorative purposes, including round, cylindrical, oval and square. Retailers could have hot water bottles made to promote their shop or store, and many were made with the shop's name, location and slogan underglazed in black. A classic example bearing the name of Harrods can be seen in the Denby Museum.

The name Bourne, Denby has always been at the forefront of the design of hot water bottles, and it is the decorative and novelty bottles which are now rare and collectable. These started to be produced just before World War I – the flat, rectangular-shaped Bungalow footwarmer first

Figure 81. Bungalow hot water bottle

appeared in the 1912 catalogue, and had an underglazed panel on the front with a picture of a bungalow and garden, together with the name Denby Stoneware

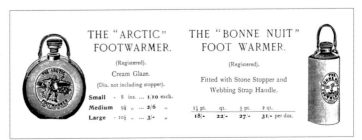

Figure 82. Catalogue illustration for footwarmers

THE "ARCTIC" FOOTWARMER.
(Registered).
Cream Glaze.
(Dia. not including stopper).

Small	-	8 ins.	...	1/10 each.
Medium	9¼	„	...	2/6	„
Large	-	10½	„	...	3/-	„

THE "BONNE NUIT" FOOT WARMER.
(Registered).
Fitted with Stone Stopper and Webbing Strap Handle.

| 1½ pt. | qt. | 3 pt. | 2 qt. |
| 18/- | 22/- | 27/- | 31/- per doz. |

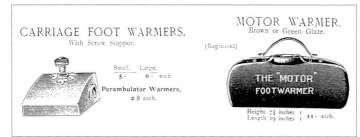

Figure 83. Catalogue illustration for carriage footwarmers and the Motor footwarmer

and a registered number. These footwarmers are not uncommon, but very rare indeed is the Motor footwarmer, which was made in either a brown or a green glaze, and, as the name suggests, was for use in the early motor cars, which of course did not have the luxury of heaters in those days.

One of the most popular, and most easily recognised, of all the Denby hot water bottles is the Gladstone Bag, which first appeared in the 1920s; it is in a dark brown colour, with a leather handle and the initials BED on the side. Much rarer is the Boudoir which was made in a blue glaze and is in the shape of a lady's handbag.

The most sought-after hot water bottles are those in the children's series – all of these are extremely rare; the Bedtime is in a cream and brown glaze and is hexagonal in shape with a clock face on it, with the hands pointing to 8 o'clock; the Dormice and the Cat and Mouse are both squarish in shape with relief pictures on the side; and the Little Folks footwarmer is a small bottle (about 6 inches square), with a child climbing into bed pictured on one side.

Figure 84. Catalogue illustration for fancy footwarmers

Figure 85. Penguin

The most attractive of the children's series were designed in the early 1930s by Donald Gilbert (the designer of many of the Denby animals and much of the Pastel series). These do not often have the name J Bourne, Denby on the underside, but the name Velray which was the name of the firm which marketed them. There are three in the series, the Squirrel (the stopper of which is a nut), the Penguin and Wilfred the Rabbit; the stoppers for these last two are the beak and the ears respectively, and are, incidentally, interchangeable. All these three were produced in different coloured glazes – blue, brown or green.

Figure 86. Wilfred

Also highly collectable are the miniature hot water bottles, which were originally sold as muff-warmers; three were produced – the Dainty, the Flat and the Egg-Shape.

Figure 87. Muff warmers (from left to right: Flat, Dainty, Egg-Shape)

10

Money Boxes

AS mentioned previously in the chapters on 'Majolica' and 'Arts and Crafts Decorative Pottery', the Denby Pottery produced money boxes. However, we need to go back to the earlier part of the 19th century to find the first examples of Denby money boxes. These tend to be quite rare and very difficult to identify as being from the Bourne factory, as all Derbyshire salt-glazed money boxes of the period bear a close similarity to each other. The money box shown in Figure 88 was most probably made at the Codnor Park Pottery, and is inscribed 'Sarah Myford February 4th 1832'. The one illustrated in Plate 2 with the inscription L. Bates was probably made circa 1840.

The Majolica money boxes were of two main types: spherical, or in the shape of a pig. The former were produced as single or double spheres, which stood on a foot or pedestal. On the top was usually an acorn finial or sometimes a bird in a contrasting white glaze. It is difficult to find such money boxes in good condition, as many owners chipped or broke the pottery whilst forcibly trying to remove the money from them.

Many stoneware potteries, for example, Prices and Powells in Bristol, and Pearsons in Chesterfield, required apprentices to produce decorative money boxes to prove that they had become master potters. We believe that this was not the case at Denby as our research has found that most of the money boxes in existence have a similar design and style of decoration.

Most of the pig money boxes are based on the design by Horace Elliott – a seated version with the money slot in the centre of its back. The earlier Elliott ones, which date from around 1900, are instantly recognisable in that they have a putty-coloured glaze with cobalt-blue sgraffito decoration, motto and date. Some of the known mottoes are

Figure 88. Money box made at the Codnor Park Pottery and dated 1832

illustrated in the chapter on 'Arts and Crafts Decorative Pottery'; we would, however, be pleased to learn of others!

Nearly all of the money boxes, and the Majolica ones in particular, were made to order and were given upon the birth of a child or some other special family occasion. The inscriptions upon them were done in gold which was applied on top of the glaze; the problem with this is, that over the years, dates and names have often worn off. Some of the Majolica money boxes also have mottoes upon them; examples are:

A little pig with roguish squint, you see the hole, please take the hint

I am a pig both quaint and funny but when I go bust you get your money

Feed me well and in your need I will prove a friend indeed

If you want me to be chummy, put a penny in my tummy.

There is a rarer version of the Majolica pig money box which first appears in the Denby advertisements of the early months of 1908. This pig is a standing version, and is extremely finely modelled, having very distinctive facial features and a twisted tail (Plate 21). There is also an elephant money box in the Majolica glaze; these, like the standing pigs, are extremely rare.

11

Advertising Wares

FROM late Victorian times, Joseph Bourne and Son produced 'Advertising Specialities'. The forerunners in this field were, of course, the ginger beer bottle and the handled bottle (more commonly called a flagon) which, from the turn of the century, were made with the name, town and trade mark printed in black underglaze. These, of course, are very common, and more details are given in the chapter on 'Bottles', but in any specialist field of collecting, certain names and pictorial trade marks are quite rare and command surprisingly high prices. Figure 89 shows an example of one of Denby's own promotional bottles.

On the old brown salt-glazed bottles, the name and address of the ginger beer maker was impressed into the bottle, either on the shoulder or the side; sometimes the trade mark was also impressed into the bottle. The white-glazed bottle with buff top was, in the early 20th century, much more popular as more

Figure 89. An example of a Denby promotional ginger beer bottle

detailed information could be incorporated into the design. The publicity material from the pottery further states 'that the printing of the name in black under the glaze is a leading feature. This forms a neat and attractive label, as well as a useful and permanent advertisement.' The name could also be added to the stopper too; these were available in stoneware, vulcanite or lignum vitae.

Amongst their 'Advertising Specialities' were jugs, mugs, ashtrays and match-strikers. These items of 'Breweriana' must have been made in profusion, but to find these today in good condition is usually a rare and costly occurrence.

Plate 23 shows a selection of advertising items from the earlier part of the 20th century; the bottle on the left is the champagne-shape ginger beer bottle and the advertising label is typical of the period, showing name, address and trade mark. Oddly enough, although there were many stoneware potteries in London, many of the Breweriana items, including bottles made at the Denby Pottery, advertise London establishments – Combe & Co. Ltd, named on the mug second from the left, was a London brewery. Catering establishments also had wares especially made for use in restaurants and cafés – the bowl in the centre advertises the House of Lyons, whilst the teapot bears the Great Northern Railway emblem and the cream pot in the foreground has the letters LNER (London & North Eastern Railway).

The pottery company resumed production of advertising wares after World War II, and Figure 90 shows a varied selection of these between the late 1940s and the 1960s. Crockery continued to be made for the railways, but of course, after nationalisation in 1948 items bore the British Railways logo. Plate 24 shows a selection of different advertising wares of the 1950s era, including a Harrods hot-water bottle, a curry paste jar and a bottle for Wilscombe Sheep Dip, but once again, the pre-

Figure 90. Catalogue illustrations of advertising specialities

dominance is for brewery-related items including ashtrays for Players Weights Cigarettes and Brickwoods Ales and Stout, a jug made for Whitbreads Brewery, a Castle Beers jug (apparently made for export to South Africa), and a Gaylord Whisky flask in the shape of a horse's head.

Over the years of our own collecting and research, we have seen a varied assortment from all aspects of commerce, including airlines (BOAC), engineering firms, food manufacturers, foundries, haulage firms, and so on.

In more recent times, mugs have been produced as promotional material. The most popular of all these were the Cadbury's Regional Mugs which were on offer in 1976. Altogether there were thirteen mugs, each, featuring pictorially, some of the main tourist attractions and famous people connected with each region. These mugs, of course, are quite common and can be purchased quite cheaply at collector's fairs and markets. The regions and pictorial features were:

1. *Scotland* – Eileen Donan Castle; Forth Bridge; Robert the Bruce Statue; James Watt; Edinburgh Castle.

PLATE 21. *Pig money boxes: three Elliott sgraffito, buff glazed, circa 1900, and three Majolica, 1908–1935*

PLATE 22. *Selection of Cottage Blue salesman's samples*

PLATE 23. *Advertising wares, 1900–30, including GNR teapot and LNER cream pot*

PLATE 24. *Advertising wares, 1940s and 1950s, including Harrods hot water bottle*

PLATE 25. *Tube-lined tobacco jars illustrating different closure patents*

PLATE 26. *Selection of tube-lined wares, circa 1925, including Eric vases (with Belt decoration), and jardinière (with Pewter glaze and Windmill decoration)*

Figure 91. Group of Cadbury's Regional Mugs, circa 1976

2. *Northumbria* – Stephenson's Locomotion; Hadrian's Wall; Durham Cathedral; Grace Darling; River Tyne.
3. *Cumbria* – Scafell Pike; Carlisle Citadel; Derwentwater; Wordsworth; River Lune, Tebay Gorge.
4. *Yorkshire, Cleveland and Humberside* – Castle Howard; Staithes; York Minster; Captain Cook; Brimham Rocks, Nidderdale.
5. *North West* – Liver Building, Liverpool; High Peak; Blackpool; Lewis Carroll; The Rows, Chester.
6. *Wales* – Llandaff Cathedral; Pentre Ifan Cromlech; Conway Castle; Dylan Thomas; Tal-y-llyn Railway.
7. *Heart of England* – Goodrich Castle; Ironbridge; Coventry Cathedral; Shakespeare; Gladstone Pottery.
8. *East Midlands* – Chatsworth House; Major Oak, Sherwood Forest; Lincoln Cathedral; Tennyson; Jew's House, Lincoln.
9. *East Anglia* – Cley-next-the-Sea; Ely Cathedral; Cambridge; Constable; Norfolk Wherry.
10. *Thames and Chilterns* – King Alfred's Statue, Wantage; Shipton-on-Cherwell; Windsor Castle; Sir Winston Churchill; White Horse, Uffington.
11. *West Country* – Polperro; Stonehenge; S.S. *Great Britain*; Sir Francis Drake; Roman Baths, Bath.
12. *London* – Hampton Court; Regents Park Zoo; Piccadilly Circus; Duke of Wellington; Greenwich.
13. *South East* – Scotney Castle; Abinger Hammer; Royal Pavilion, Brighton; William Caxton; Seven Sisters, Sussex.

12

Tobacco Jars

ALTHOUGH smoking in public is now largely considered to be an anti-social practice, the fact remains that the collecting of smoking-related artefacts is very much on the increase. The Denby Pottery, over the years, and particularly in the 1930s, produced a multitude of ashtrays of different designs, shapes and sizes; details of these can be found in the chapters on 'Advertising Wares' and 'Animals and Novelties'.

Tobacco jars are the most popular with collectors of 'Smokiana' and Denby were certainly in the forefront of design and production of these. The 1919 catalogue illustrates a selection of nine different tobacco jars, three with airtight

Figure 92. Catalogue illustrations of tobacco jars

lids with brass pressers, and six with loose lids. They came in assorted colours, some with rough centres; they were also available in Denby Colours, Chocolate and Danesby, that is, Majolica. All shapes were named – of particular interest are Virginia, Raleigh and Bale. Many of the tobacco jars made at the pottery do not bear the name Denby on the unglazed base; the name most commonly found is 'Aonian'. This registered trade mark was used by the firm of A Oppenheimer & Co., who were established in 1860 and who traded from Finsbury Square in London EC2. Their advertising pulls of the mid-1920s illustrate a whole range of different stoneware tobacco jars, in a variety of designs and colours, by the three leading producers of the time (Joseph Bourne & Son's Denby Pottery, Lovatt & Lovatt of Langley Mill, near Nottingham, and Doulton and Co. of Lambeth, London).

Some of the attractive range of designs which came from the Denby Pottery are illustrated in Plate 27 which shows the original advertising material. Many of these were made in the current production glazes of the time, for example, TJ 1/A (College) and TJ 24 (not pictured) were in the Majolica glaze, TJ 4/A and 5/A were in the Rainbow glaze (similar to Majolica), TJ 8/C was in the Orient glaze (originally called Brown and Blue Orient when it was introduced), and, numbers 9 to 20 all exhibited the tube-lining style of decoration (9, 10 and 15 – Floral; 11 – Rosette; 12 and 13 – Medallion; 14 and 18 – Festoon; 17 – Jewelled [in Hammered Pewter]; and 20 – Shamrock).

The rarest of all the tube-lined tobacco jars is the Golfer (TJ 19/C) which has a picture of the golfer on the tee, together with a band depicting the fairway and the flag, but the crowning glory of this piece is the golf ball top, which is also made of pottery and is part of the closure device. These jars are very rare indeed – an antiques dealer in London, specialising in 'Golfiana' has only seen one of these in twenty years of trading!

All of the different tobacco jars had names which befitted their shape:

1. College	2. Imperial (Low)	3. Princess
4. Pekoe (like the teapot!)	5. Classic	6. Barrel
7. Tub	8. Casket	9/10. Cabinet
11. Embassy	12. Lobby	13. Sandhurst
14. Regent	15. Ambassador	16. Imperial (Tall)
17. Senator	18. Rajah	19. Sports
20. City	21. Cavendish	

It is interesting to note that, in addition to the Orient Ware glaze, some of the tobacco jars at this time, circa 1925, were also available in the Electric Blue glaze (approximately three or four years before the realisation of the large-scale commercial potential of these two art pottery ranges).

T.T. Fitting—When the knob is screwed the two plates are drawn together, the rubber band being pressed against the sides of the jar.

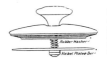

Patent Invisible Fitting – The screwing of the knob turns the metal bar against stops inside the jar, drawing the lid down until it makes an airtight joint with the rubber washer.

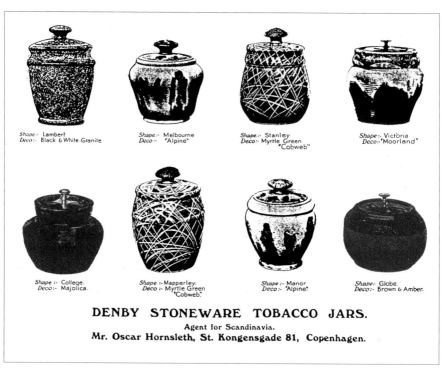

Shape :- Lambert
Deco :- Black & White-Granite.

Shape :- Melbourne
Deco :- 'Alpine'

Shape :- Stanley
Deco :- Myrtle Green
'Cobweb"

Shape :- Victoria
Deco :- 'Moorland'

Shape :- College.
Deco :- Majolica.

Shape :- Mapperley.
Deco :- Myrtle Green
'Cobweb."

Shape :- Manor
Deco :- 'Alpine'

Shape :- Globe.
Deco :- Brown & Amber.

DENBY STONEWARE TOBACCO JARS.

Agent for Scandinavia.
Mr. Oscar Hornsleth, St. Kongensgade 81, Copenhagen.

Figure 93. Catalogue illustrations of the TT fitting and the Patent Invisible fitting (top), and the tobacco jars made for export (bottom)

    One other point of interest in connection with the tobacco jars is the variation in the different patent lid fittings. The most common was the Oxidised Copper or Brass Triangle (see 5/A and 18/A), but also available was the TT Fitting (see 2/B and 11/B). The most ingenious, however, was the Patent Invisible Fitting (see 8/C and 9/C) which had ceramic knobs. Each of the latter two patents is illustrated in Figure 93.

    Tobacco jar manufacture continued through the 1930s, and although the tube-lined series was discontinued (this design feature was considered to be less fashionable), new shapes were introduced. The illustrations show that some of the glazes were quite revolutionary, particularly the black and white granite and the myrtle green 'cobweb'. Many of these designs were made primarily for the export market, particularly for Scandinavia.

Also in the 1930s a small amount of novelty tobacco jars, featuring animals, were made; a striking example is one with penguins around the body of the jar (this one was undoubtedly designed by Gilbert – see the chapter on 'Danesby Ware'). The tobacco jar shown in Figure 94 is in an Epic Green glaze, with the novelty dog Buttons as the finial. As there are no catalogue illustrations available, it is difficult to guess exactly how many were produced, and also how many different types are in existence.

Figure 94. Tobacco jar with the novelty dog Buttons as the finial

Production of tobacco jars resumed for a short time after World War II; by now the shape had become more standardised and the range of colours was more limited – browns, greens and creams seem to have predominated. Some were made in the Tally-Ho design (see the chapter 'The Effects of Wartime'), with the hunting scenes in applied decoration around the central band; these, however, were mainly made for American export.

The only one of the post-war tobacco jars which was strikingly different was the one in the shape of a barrel with an applied relief decoration of 'The Snuff-Taker' on the front.

Finally, in connection with the topic of 'Smokiana', again, with the pipe-smoker in mind, the Pottery did make pipe rests in the shape of 1940s armchairs and settees.

13

Vases and Bowls

THE Joseph Bourne pottery at Denby had not really gained any recognition for its decorative art wares in the first 100 years of its existence. However, attempts were made in the Edwardian era to produce functional pottery with more artistic shapes and/or more than one or two basic all-over glazes. The 1907 catalogue introduced flower tubes (plain and rough-centred), and bulb bowls with more imaginative shapes. All the bowls and plant pots had names attached to their shapes, for example, Oriel, Pembroke, Mentone and Orchid. The 1912 catalogue first saw the appearance of the owl jug in assorted colours (these original jugs are very rare, as most of those which come up for sale today were made in the 1930s), and the range of shapes of bulb bowls was extended to include Rose, Tavistock, Arundel, Killarney, Carisbrooke and Oriental (this shape continued through well into the 1930s).

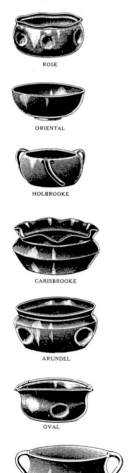

The range of vases and bulb bowls was further extended in 1919 (Figure 95), and some interesting and unique shapes were produced including Gothic, Capitol, Gondola, Holbrooke and Pekin. A variety of plain-coloured plant pots was also available – these included the very classical-sounding Marathon, Corinth

Figure 95. Illustrations from the 1919 catalogue (see also top of facing page)

Orchid

and Athenian, as well as the Gipsy kettle, which was cauldron-shaped and had three protruding 'feet'. It is interesting to note that small plant pots and bowls were, in the earlier part of this century, called fern pots. Even in this range some fascinating

Gipsy kettle

shapes existed; of particular note are the Keswick, Launcelot and Marmion.

The forerunners of the true decorative period of the 1930s first appeared in the mid-1920s; some of the named shapes of this period were adopted later in the true Electric Blue and Orient Ware ranges including Stancliffe, Hardwick and Sicilian.

The rarest and most unique of all the bulb bowls must certainly be 'The Poet Series'. These, according to the catalogue of the mid-1920s, had a glazed powder blue outside (Pastel Blue) with myrtle green inside, but had a raised design of the flower in natural colours, with the wording in raised lettering (tube-lining), on the opposite side. There were three bowls in the series:

1. Daffodil
    'And then my heart with pleasure fills,
    And dances with the daffodils'

    – *Wordsworth*

or

    'Daffodils,
    That come before the swallow dares, and take
    The winds of March with Beauty'

    – *Shakespeare*

Figure 96. Catalogue illustrations of bulb bowls

83

THE POET SERIES OF BULB BOWLS

Glazed Powder Blue outside, Myrtle Green inside. Raised design of Flower in Natural Colours on one side.
Wording in Raised Letters

380 "Daffodil"
Sizes : 7, 8 in. diam.

381 "Narcissus"
Sizes : 7, 8 in. diam.

382 "Snowdrop"
Sizes : 7, 8 in. diam.

Figure 97. Catalogue illustrations of 'The Poet Series' of bulb bowls

303

305

307

343

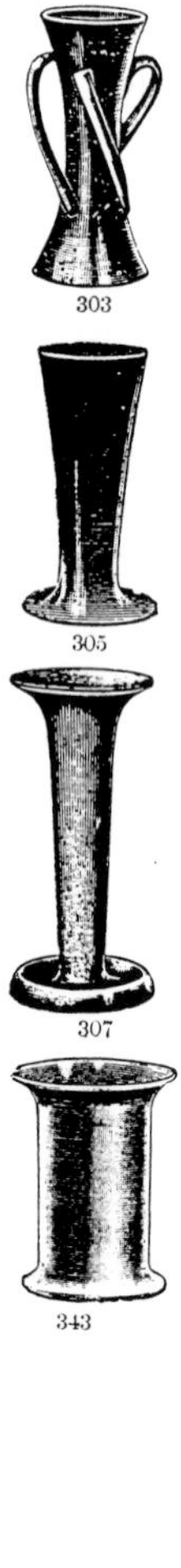

2. Narcissus
'Narcissi, the fairest among them all,
Who gaze on their eyes in stream's recess
'Till they die of their own dear loveliness'
— *Shelley*

3. Snowdrop (with wording around the top)
'Chaste Snowdrop venturous harbinger of
spring' — *Wordsworth.*

By the year 1912, Denby had extended their range
of plain-coloured glazed vases; new shapes were
introduced in addition to the flower tube. A variation of the plain tube was green, with a white
roughened centre. All the new shapes had names, for
example, Paxton, Trumpet, Sweet Pea tube, Column, Park, Cleopatra, Obelisk and Handled (this
latter one had 'twisted' handles and was originally
introduced in the Majolica range).

Figure 98. Illustrations from the 1912 catalogue.
Left column (from top): Handled, Trumpet, Sweet pea tube,
Park; right column (from top): Paxton, Ivanhoe, Column,
Cleopatra

304

306

308

310

TOBACCO JARS

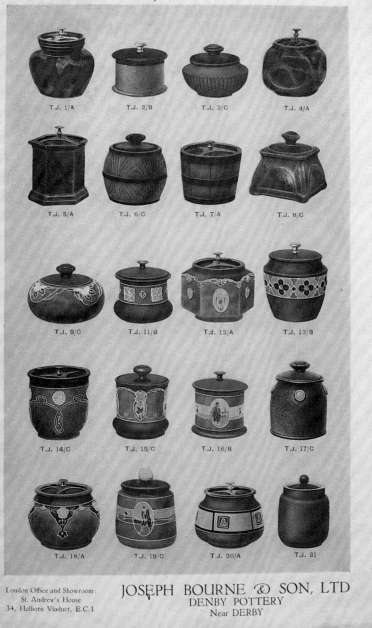

PLATE 27. *Illustrated advertisement for Denby tobacco jars, circa 1925*

14

Tube-Lined Wares

THESE fine, under-rated and often unrecognised wares started to be produced around 1924; again the name 'Danesby' is associated with the range, which the catalogues described as 'Danesby Decorated Stoneware'.

This range of decorative pottery may well have been instigated by the production of an ornate commemorative piece made for the 1924 British Empire Exhibition; it is not known how many of these pieces were made, but it is extremely rare to find examples of them for sale. The piece consists of a stepped plinth, at the corners of which are four lions couchant, and in the centre is a globe of the world with the continents picked out with tube-lining (this technique was widely used in decorative pottery in the 1920s and 1930s and was applied to the pots in a similar way to decorating a cake using an icing bag). The piece also features a crown and is inscribed 'Reproduction of the Gold Casket presented to H.M. King at the opening of the Exhibition April 23rd. 1924 – manufactured by J. Bourne and Son Ltd. Denby Pottery, near Derby' (Figure 99 and Plate 29).

Figure 99. Mark on base of 1924 British Empire Exhibition piece

The production of decorative vases and bowls began in the middle of the decade and pieces were available in a variety of colours (Royal Blue, Matt Brown, Celeste, Amethyst, Yellow, Ruby, and Pewter), and also in different combinations of these. The tube-lined decorative motifs included Carnival, Rosette, Gothic, Lunar, Festoon, Floral and Belt. The range of shapes was modified in 1925 to include the Celtic vase, Trent, Repton and Avon bowls, and the number of motifs was extended to include Windmill, Panel and Heart.

This range of 'Danesby Decorated Stoneware' also exhibits the first large-scale use of geographical names for the different shaped pieces, a trend which continued throughout the art-ware production in the 1930s and early 1940s.

Butterfly Ware

Although not exactly tube-lined decoration, it is worth mentioning the three pieces of Butterfly Ware (shown in Plate 31) which are to be seen in the Museum at Denby Pottery. Their origin and date of production still remain something of an enigma; we have no evidence as to the existence of other items. One suggestion is that there may be a connection between the Denby Butterfly Ware and the Royal Torquay Pottery which produced a similar design, but in brown and cream-coloured glazes, between 1910 and 1930.

PLATE 28. *Richly-glazed, tube-lined ware:*
Baslow jug and Peveril vase, early 1930s

PLATE 29. *Commemorative presentation globe*
made for 1924 British Empire Exhibition

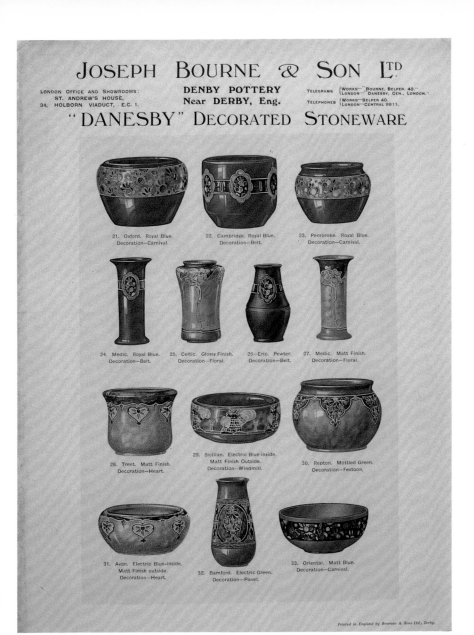

Printed in England by Bemrose & Sons Ltd., Derby.

PLATE 30. *Illustrated catalogue page for Danesby Decorated Stoneware, circa 1925*

15

Danesby Ware

THE General Strike of 1926 and the subsequent Depression led to many companies, including Denby, facing a bleak future. In 1931, refurbishment of equipment and updating of processes was undertaken to ensure the company's survival. It was around this time that the Denby Pottery concentrated on extending its limited range of art wares which had begun after World War I. The success of this was mainly due to the arrival of one or two leading designers to Denby, the most influential of whom was Donald Gilbert.

Most of the art wares bear the name Danesby Ware, which appears on the bases of the decorative pieces. To many people, the style of the 'signature' may have a look of familiarity about it, as it comes from the hand of Albert Colledge, whose signature appears on the underside of pieces of the Greenwheat range of tableware. It was he, under the direction of Norman Wood, who set up the art-ware production at Denby.

The name Danesby remains somewhat enigmatic – the first known appearance of this name associated with the Pottery is as early as 1886 in Joseph Bourne and Son's advertisement in the *Pottery Gazette*. At the turn of the century it was used by Joseph Bourne as the London office telegram code; it has also been seen impressed (see mark L in the glossary of marks later in the book) on the bases of a few pieces of Denby Majolica Ware (circa 1900-20). There is one school of thought which suggests that the Denby locality was, in earlier times, called Danesby, but so far this is unsubstantiated (there is a road in the neighbouring village of Kilburn called Danesby Rise!).

Electric Blue and Orient Ware

These two ranges have become the most popular and easily purchased of all the 1930s Denby decorative art wares. They were produced at a time when there was a penchant for studio-type decorative wares with eye-catching glazes.

Both the Electric Blue and Orient Ware glazes, however, were in existence several years before they were introduced as a range of art wares; they first appeared around 1925 in an interesting and attractive range of 'fancy glazed and decorated bowls', some of which are extremely rare today, for example, the Casket, which was available in the Orient Ware (and Pastel Blue) glazes with a tube-lined windmill decoration, and the Stancliffe bowl which could be

Figure 100. Electric Blue teaset, circa 1928

purchased, not only in either glaze, but also in a hammered pewter with a jewelled effect. We also have evidence that the decorative glazes found their way on to some of the domestic items, possibly to make them more special, or to be given as presentation pieces, for example, an Electric Blue teapot exists with gold personalisation and a 1928 date; there is also a teaset made at a similar date, consisting of teapot, hot-water jug, milk jug and sugar basin.

The Denby catalogues of the 1930s suggest that the ranges of Electric Blue and Orient Ware had similar shapes, but there is a wide variety of individual shapes within each range, although some overlapping does exist. The full list of shapes and designs reads rather like a gazetteer of the Peak District – Tideswell, Bakewell, Baslow, Tansley, Crich and Rowsley are just a handful of the names of Derbyshire villages. A few of the names described the shapes of the individual items – such as Sweet Pea tube, Phial, Trumpet, Owl – and others had names which were connected with other geographical locations - Swiss, Oriental, Sicilian, Pembroke and Torino.

From the catalogues of the time, it can be seen that many of the shapes were available in different sizes, for example, the Peveril vase was available in four different sizes, the largest being 18 inches high and was retailed at 30/- (£1.50)! Certainly, evidence would suggest that during the relatively short period over which these wares were produced (mainly between 1928–38), the ranges were extended and modified, for example, the Orient Ware Trumpet vase is ridged towards the top; the tall candlestick in this design is a different shape from the Electric Blue, and many of the Orient Ware pieces have additional incised relief decoration. Evidence would also suggest that some of the shapes which were catalogued as being produced in both Orient Ware and Electric Blue are rare in

PLATE 31. *Butterfly Ware*

PLATE 32. *Danesby Electric Blue (from left to right: Back row – Alton, Birchover, Castleton, Crich, Tansley; Front row – Swiss, Ilam, Goblet candlestick)*

PLATE 33. *Danesby Electric Blue including Wingfield, Peveril (three sizes), Tideswell, Longnor, Rowsley, Low candlestick*

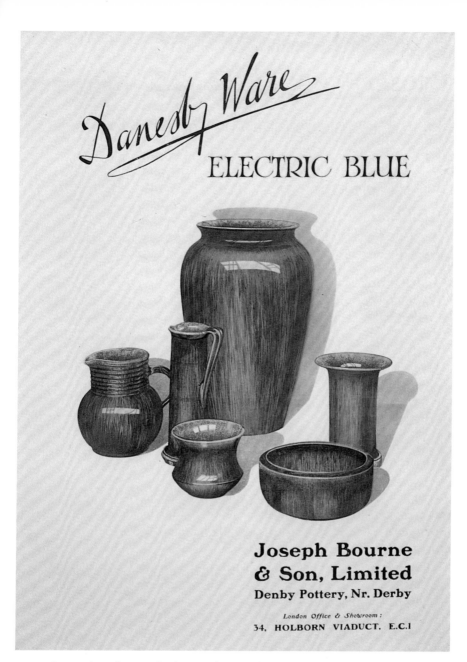

PLATE 34. *Illustrated title page from catalogue for Danesby Electric Blue*

FANCY GLAZED & DECORATED BOWLS

335 "Oriental"
Colours : Electric Blue
Orient Ware
Sizes : 6, 7, 8 in. diam.

377 "Stanton"
Colour : Meadow Green
Sizes : 7, 8 in. diam.

374 "Parwich"
Colours : Electric Blue
Orient Ware
Sizes : 7, 8, 9 in. diam.

373 "Beeley"
Colour : Electric Blue
Sizes : 7, 8 in. diam

372 "Hardwick"
Colours : Electric Blue
Orient Ware
Size : 8 in. diam.

353 "Sicilian"
Colours : Electric Blue
Also Windmill Decoration
(See Casket shape below)
Sizes : 6, 7, 8 in. diam.

375 "Stancliffe"
Colours : Electric Blue
Orient Ware
Hammered Pewter
(Jewelled)
Sizes : 6, 10 in. diam.

376 "Avocca," Handled
Colours : Electric Blue
Orient Ware
Size : 9¼ in. diam.

379 "Casket"
Colour : Orient Ware
(Windmill Decoration)
Size : 11 in. Long

378 "Cabinet"
Colours : Brown and Blue
(Floral Decoration)
Meadow Green
(Floral Decoration)
Sizes : 7, 8 in. diam.

Figure 101. Catalogue illustrations showing Electric Blue and Orient Ware shapes

the latter glaze, such as Middleton, Brassington, Ilam, Hardwick, Castleton, Derwent and Elephant bookends.

An interesting, apparently non-catalogued series of smaller pieces in Orient Ware includes small, squat vases with an incised 'Greek key-pattern' around the rim, and also a set of four ashtrays in the shape of a heart, diamond, spade and club (presumably designed to be used when playing cards!). There are other ranges similar to Orient Ware, but in different coloured glazes. One such range is Meadow Green, but the number of shapes available was much more limited than the Orient Ware. As so few pieces of this ware appear for sale at auctions and antiques fairs and markets, one can only assume that the range was made for only a short duration during the 1930s.

There are also other variants in existence, including a brown and creamy glaze which was called Moorland, but sadly there are no known catalogues in existence, so it is impossible to describe the availability of shapes. One other variant of the Orient Ware glaze is the yellowy-green vase shown in Plate 39, but it is thought that this may have been a prototype.

Antique Green

A much-less extensive range of art wares in the 1930s was the Danesby Antique Green range. This was really a natural progression from the tube-lined wares of the 1920s. The glaze and range of shapes were entirely different from Electric Blue and Orient Ware, but once again they all had Derbyshire place names such as Matlock, Brailsford, Pentrich, Hassop, Milford and Duffield. Items in this range are not nearly so common as the Orient Ware and Electric Blue, which can probably be explained by the fact that only seventeen different items and shapes were marketed.

Regent Pastel and Pastel Blue

By far the most popular of all the Danesby Ware ranges (apart from the animals and novelties) are the Pastel ranges. Both ranges have a basic grey 'putty', semi-matt glaze (known in the trade as 'suet') with moulded relief decorations of flora, fauna, and also typically Art Deco abstract subjects, and cloud formations.

The designer of most of these ranges was Donald Gilbert, who was a young free-lance designer and sculptor and was enticed to Denby circa 1930. He was born at Burcot in Worcestershire in 1900 and was the son of sculptor Walter Gilbert. He studied sculpture at the Birmingham Central School of Art, the Royal College of Art and the Royal Academy, and his main tutor for a time was Sir Alfred Gilbert, who is most famed for his statue of Eros in London's Piccadilly Circus. Donald Gilbert's main forte was his production of animal sculptures – it is certainly this talent which is very much in evidence in his work at Denby, both in the Regent Pastel and Pastel Blue ranges, and also in his large animal models (see later in the following sections). After he had finished his design work at the pottery around 1933–34, he had an exhibition in 1934 at the Wertheim Gallery, Burlington Gardens, London W1, which largely consisted of animal sculptures in stone, marble and wood; these included African elephant, rhinoceros, lion cub, antelope, kicking horse, turkey, monkey, and so on, and there were also portrait busts of famous people, including the composer Sir Edward Elgar. Donald Gilbert also exhibited at the Royal Academy, Glasgow Institute and Paris Salon.

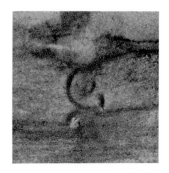

Figure 102. Incised 'G' (for Gilbert) sometimes found on Danesby Regent Pastel

Sadly, the line drawings in the 1930s catalogues illustrating the Regent Pastel and Pastel Blue, do no justice whatsoever to Gilbert's design skills. It

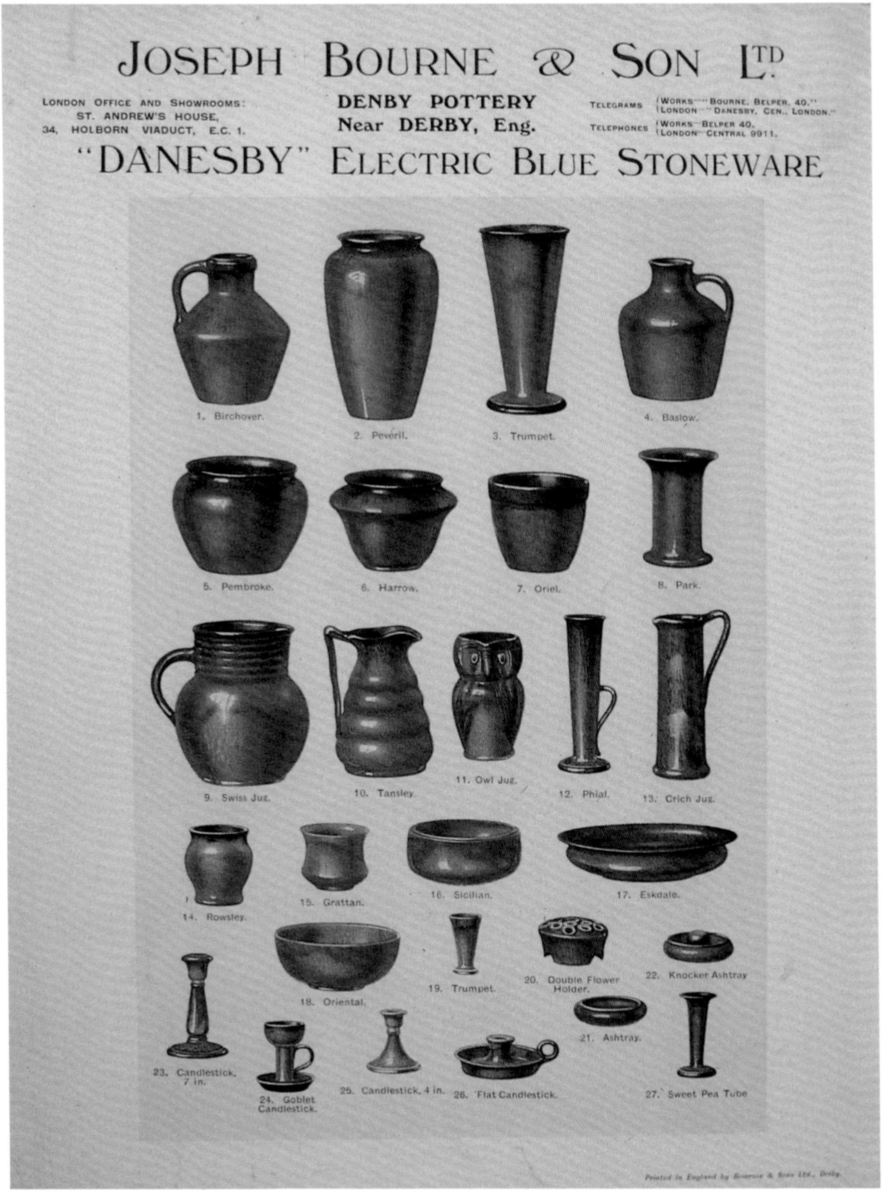

PLATE 35. *Illustrated catalogue page for Danesby Electric Blue, circa 1930*

PLATE 36. *Tansley jug and Monsal vase in Orient Ware (shiny glaze)*

PLATE 37. *Danesby Orient Ware (from left to right: Back row – Birchover, Hucklow, Castleton, Howden; Front row – Name not known, Marmaduke rabbit, Tray candlestick)*

PLATE 38. *Danesby Orient Ware (from left to right: Back row – Riber, Thorpe, Wynne, Hopton, Derwent, Chevin; Front row – Stancliffe)*

is very rare indeed to actually find pieces signed with his signature in full; Figure 102 shows a close-up of the tan-coloured glaze typically found at the base of Regent Pastel pieces and illustrates an incised 'G' (for Gilbert). Other pieces, such as bookends, have GILBERT SCULPTOR printed on the underside next to Bourne, Denby and the Danesby Ware 'signature'.

The range of vases, jugs and bowls is identical in both the Regent Pastel (which leans towards the browns and greens) and the Pastel Blue (which, as the name implies, has a predominance of blue). As with the Electric Blue and Orient Ware ranges, the ranges have names connected with a geographical region; the first twenty-four items (excepting one) all have names appertaining to the Lake District, for example, Kendal, Grasmere, Ambleside, Windermere, Skiddaw, and so on. The odd one out is DP19 (short for Danesby Pastel), which is the Netherlea vase (Netherlea was the name of the large house in the village of Holbrook, near to Denby, where the Bourne-Wheelers – the owners of the Pottery – lived until 1942). Most of the first twenty-one pieces in the catalogue are of an abstract design.

The most spectacular vases in the Pastel ranges really exhibited Gilbert's excellent portrayal of animals and birds – the finest pieces being the Bowness vase (featuring swimming fish on the body of the vase with otter handles), the Dalton vase (with swimming fish and aquatic plants), the Giraffe vase, the Walton vase (with kingfishers and bulrushes), the Flamingo vase, and the Swallow vase.

We have discovered a lot of Donald Gilbert's work at Denby which does not appear in any of the catalogues; it is difficult to ascertain whether these were specially commissioned individual pieces or whether they formed part of a limited range of more expensive and exclusive art-ware pieces. Into this category comes a series of pieces which feature penguins; there is the large vase and ashtray (Plate 55), and also a tobacco jar. Another stunning piece is the Kingfisher bowl; this, in particular, illustrates the way in which Gilbert captured perfectly the anatomical realism.

Also worthy of special note are three unusual, but very striking, pieces of Gilbert's skilful design called Cleopatra vase, Cleopatra bowl and Cleopatra ashtray. Once again, the catalogue illustrations give no indication whatsoever of the eye-catching beauty of these items, although the Cleopatra bowl can be seen in Plate 52.

Animals (attributed to Gilbert)

The Regent Pastel and Pastel Blue catalogues also contain a section which contains some fine animal pottery 'sculptures' by Gilbert. These, like the Kingfisher bowl, are beautifully modelled and some were only available in Pastel

Blue. The range includes Penguin, Sea Lion, Drake, Cat, Stork, plus a miscellany of smaller items such as Fish ashtray, Lovebird, Duck(s), set of Geese (which were marketed in boxed form), Mother Goose (14 inches high), and Teddy Bear.

Rabbits always make popular subjects, and these are described in the chapter on 'Animals and Novelties'. However, there is one 'sculpture' which is a most imposing piece; that is the Mushroom Group, which features two large mushrooms, complete with gills on the underside, and having two small rabbits sitting on top of the larger mushroom (Plate 51).

Another magnificent piece of Gilbert's work is the Sun Fish, which was not only marketed as a decorative object, but was also produced as a lamp and as a garden fountain (see the next section 'Garden Pottery'). Also impressive is the Geese 'sculpture', which, like the Sun Fish, was also marketed as a lamp; the piece shown in Plate 58 has its original shade!

Bookends

These are extremely popular and collectable. Most of the range was designed by Gilbert; the full known list is:

1. Fish	2. Fluttering Bird	3. Lovebird	4. Rabbits	5. Elephant
6. Dog	7. Terrier	8. Seagull	9. Pelican	10. Kingfisher

Although most of these were made in either the Regent Pastel or Pastel Blue glazes, some, particularly the Rabbits, Elephant and Fish, were also produced in a matt green; the latter was also available in the Greenland glaze (a matt white). The Seagull, Pelican and Kingfisher are the rarest of all the bookends.

Garden Pottery

A special range of art pottery with emphasis on animals and birds was produced at Denby around the mid-1930s. The advertising material of the time states:

THERE'S JOY IN MAKE-BELIEVE

Picture to yourself a corner of your garden made gay with these charming figures! Aloof yet sociable, the penguin mounts guard on the shore of the tiny pond. Frogs are basking at the water's edge. The leafy arbour is lively with squirrels, whose chatter you can almost hear . . .

Yes, there is joy in make-believe, and there are other figures, too, who will take the reins of your imagination. Then yours will be a garden of Romance, a little kingdom of colourful subjects, a source of continual delight to the children.

One point you must watch, however, when you buy garden figures, is resistance

PLATE 39. *Rare decorative glazes of the 1930s, including Meadow Green (centre) and Moorland (right)*

PLATE 40. *Danesby Antique Green Ware (from left to right: Heath [4½inches], Brailsford, Totley, Heath [3½inches])*

PLATE 41. *Casket in Pastel Blue with tube-lined Windmill decoration, late 1920s*

PLATE 42. *Danesby Pastel Blue (from left to right: Kirkstone, Walton, Grasmere)*

PLATE 43. *Danesby Pastel Blue (from left to right: Honistor, Thirlmere, Netherlea)*

PLATE 44. *Danesby Regent Pastel (from left to right: Ilkley, Dandelion, Swallow)*

PLATE 45. *Danesby Pastel Blue Dalton vase*

PLATE 46. *Danesby Regent Pastel Flamingo vase by Gilbert*

PLATE 47. *Danesby Regent Pastel (from left to right: Walton, Thorne, Otley, Trent, Catkin, with Geese spill vase at front)*

PLATE 48. *Danesby Regent Pastel (from left to right: Lodore bowl, Netherlea, Rydal, Penrith)*

to the action of the weather. Our figures are strong and durable, being specially made to withstand sun, wind, and rain. You will be satisfied with Danesby Ware, it is REAL pottery.

Again, the unique design features of Gilbert are in evidence in most of the range, some of which are quite spectacular pieces of art pottery. Sadly, most of these are extremely rare; could it be that they did not weather the elements too well? Figure 103 gives an idea of the appearance of the range but does not really do justice to these fine pieces of pottery. The most spectacular pieces in the range are the Penguin, Duck, Squirrel, Swan and Geese bowl.

A very unusual piece in the Garden Pottery series is the Pedestal which is a cone-shaped item, with a brown textured rock-like, semi-matt glaze, about 15 inches high, designed to support the Sun Fish bowl and fountain. Also belonging to the Garden Pottery series, but not shown in the catalogues are the large jugs (see Plate 59) having a 'putty' glaze with large tan-coloured swirls and a tan-coloured band around the base (which is very much a hallmark of Gilbert's design and is not dissimilar to the Regent Pastel glaze).

Figure 103. Illustrations from a promotional leaflet for Garden Pottery

PLATE 49. *Danesby Pastel Blue Kingfisher bowl and Kingfisher bookends by Gilbert*

PLATE 50. *Danesby Regent Pastel Woodland vase*

PLATE 51. *Danesby Sylvan Pastel Mushroom Group with Rabbits*

PLATE 52. *Group of Danesby Regent Pastel and Pastel Blue,*
including Cleopatra bowl, Delphinium jug, Antelope vase

PLATE 53. *Danesby Regent Pastel Lovebird bookends with Bowness vase in centre*

PLATE 54. *Danesby Pastel Seagull bookends and Penguin ashtray*

Returning to the Danesby Ware Pastel ranges, if one closely examines the catalogues of the 1930s, it becomes evident what a productive period this was for the art-ware side of Denby Pottery. Regular revisions were made of these catalogues, mainly because new designs and ranges of pottery were continually being introduced, and the ones already in existence were constantly being updated. At some stage during the decade the Regent Pastel and Pastel Blue ranges were described under the heading of Sylvan Pastel (Sylvan Pastel was yet another glaze variation in itself – it was a semi-matt pale green). This glaze proved to be less popular than either the Regent or the Blue and eventually the catalogues described the series of art ware as 'Danesby Ware Pastel'.

Featherstone Ware

In the second half of the thirties' decade, the Regent Pastel range was extended to include Featherstone Ware. The design features on this ware certainly bear more than a close resemblance to the work of Alice Teichner (see the section following on Tyrolean Ware)

The series, in common with the rest of the Danesby Ware, had names of shapes linked with a common geographical theme. All the twenty different pieces, with the exception of number 9, had names of Scottish locations, for example Sutherland, Falkirk, Perth, Callander, Hamilton, Dundee, and so on. Number 9 is called the Brailsford jug; this is, once again, a Derbyshire location.

Some of the shapes were strikingly different from anything else that the Denby Pottery had created and certainly the nature of the applied decoration was quite revolutionary for the 1930s. This of course, was the very distinctive style of Miss Teichner. They consisted of very minimalist ideas suggestive of flowers, trees and leaves, often in a vivid mustard-coloured glaze.

The odd ones out in the range were numbers 18 and 19 which were pieces in the shapes of rather comical-looking fish, one in the form of an ashtray (Moray) and the other as a pair of bookends (Dundee).

The Featherstone series was also available in a shiny, greyish-blue glaze.

Floral Pastel

Another of the Danesby Ware Pastel ranges, produced later in the 1930s decade, was the Floral Pastel. Again, as with the Featherstone range, it is almost certain that the designs were influenced by Alice Teichner.

The shapes too, all have Scottish names and are all different from the Featherstone ones. Names include Thurso, Galloway, Forfar, Paisley and Arbroath, but strangely, there is one anomaly – Perth is used in both ranges but describes totally different-shaped pieces. In Featherstone it is given to a rather bulbous, two-handled vase; in Floral Pastel it belongs to a round, flat-topped posy bowl.

There are eighteen decorative pieces in all in the Floral Pastel range, mainly vases, but also bowls and wall pockets. The attractive feature about the range is that the decoration of flowers is in deep relief, on a greyish/putty-coloured ground. Flowers represented include anemone, delphinium, fuchsia, hollyhocks, Canterbury bells, foxglove and Michaelmas daisies.

Ivory Pastel

Another quite interesting series that was added to the Pastel range later in the decade, was Ivory Pastel. As the name suggests, the principal glaze colour was a semi-matt ivory colour with a moulded relief floral panels. The coarse background texture to the panels is a chocolate brown colour, with the stylised flowers in buttery-yellow and the stems and leaves in a sage green.

Some interesting and different shapes were available in the limited series of twelve but, different from the rest of the Pastel ranges, the shapes were not named, they were merely described in the catalogues as No. 1, No. 2, and so on.

Two bowls were made (Nos 11 and 12); the former of these was quite different in that it portrayed, in relief, a pastoral scene with stylised trees and other vegetation, together with a young deer.

As with most of the Denby decorative ranges of the 1930s, it is possible to find non-catalogued items; one such item in the Ivory Pastel series was a small lamp base. There is also a less popular version of the Ivory Pastel in which the relief decoration is in blues and pinks.

Tyrolean

A designer called Alice Teichner, who was an Austrian refugee, joined the Denby Pottery around 1936. Her designs were remarkable and distinctive and were really 20 years ahead of her time. Many general antique collectors have been surprised to learn that pieces designed by her were made before World War II, and not in the early 1950s, as the style of pottery seems to suggest.

The style of her work is heavy, often with thick rims and handles and with applied loops and ribs; it has the appearance of studio pottery. Miss Teichner apparently had a sound knowledge of glaze formulation and experimented with different coloured glazes, the most striking being a yellowy-orange. The decorative wares directly attributable to her are the most easily identifiable as they have the words 'Made in England' and the monogram AT.

PLATE 55. *Danesby Regent Pastel designs by Gilbert (from left to right: Penguin ashtray, Penguin, Penguin vase)*

PLATE 56. *Drake by Gilbert*

PLATE 57. *Danesby Pastel Sun Fish and Fish bookends*

PLATE 58. *Geese lamp with contemporary shade*

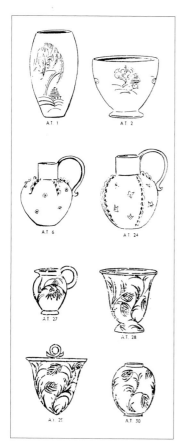

Figure 104. Some of the shapes available in Tyrolean Ware

Unlike most of the Danesby Ware decorative ranges, the Alice Teichner shapes (and there are some 60 documented ones) do not have names linked with a common theme; the catalogues of the late 1930s and early 1940s merely have the overall title of 'Tyrolean' and the numbers AT1, AT2, and so on (some of the more common pieces are illustrated in Plates 66 and 68, and some of the more distinctive pieces are shown in Plates 67 and 69). Pottery designed by her could be purchased in a variety of coloured glazes, including blue, sepia, old gold, green and even Orient blue.

It is only recently that the impact of her design skills at Denby Pottery is being fully appreciated. Closer examination of the Danesby Ware ranges suggests that her influence was more far-reaching than was originally thought. We have already implied that she probably had some input into the Denby Grey range; there is no doubt that she designed the Featherstone Ware (which forms part of the Regent Pastel range). The Floral Pastel range too, almost certainly bears some of the hallmarks of her design skills, and also, many of the animal novelties (in particular the terrier dogs, goose ashtray, and Puck ashtray) bear her monogram and distinctive creative features.

Denby Grey

There are many questions still to be answered about this range of decorative wares, as there are no known catalogues of the shapes available and no documentary evidence about the designs.

The pottery was produced in a shiny grey glaze with a cobalt blue sgraffito decoration, rather similar to the German Westphalian wares. The very chunky appearance of the designs, coupled with thick rims and handles, would almost certainly suggest that they belong to Alice Teichner, and were probably her first designs undertaken at Denby, circa 1936–37.

Pieces are clearly marked with the words 'Denby Grey' and the usual Danesby

Ware mark. The colour of the unglazed underside is also quite different; instead of the usual buff/cream colour, it has a reddish, almost speckled appearance. Some examples of Denby Grey are shown in Plates 70 and 73.

Greenland

Another of the 'Pastel' style designs of Danesby Ware is Greenland which has an icy-white semi-matt glaze with stylised floral (and fauna) designs incised into the body of the pots. This range uses mainly Australian geographical names for the different design shapes, such as Sydney, Canberra, Darwin and Adelaide. One or two shapes were 'borrowed' from other series of Danesby Ware, for example Forfar jug and Stonehaven bowl.

The Townsville vase is in some ways similar in design to the Dalton vase (in the Regent Pastel and Pastel Blue ranges), in that it has a decoration of fish and aquatic plants; the Ballater mug has a delightful decoration of a rabbit and toadstools.

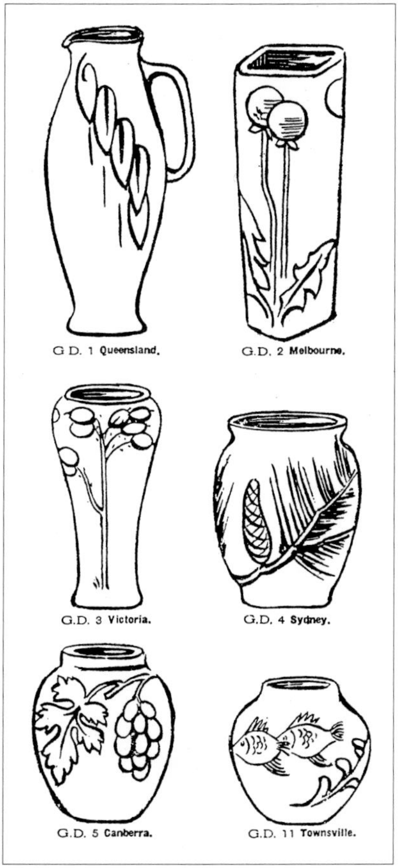

G.D. 1 Queensland.

G.D. 2 Melbourne.

G.D. 3 Victoria.

G.D. 4 Sydney.

G.D. 5 Canberra.

G.D. 11 Townsville.

Figure 105. Some of the shapes available in the Greenland series

Figure 106. Greenland vase

PLATE 59. *Garden Pottery*

PLATE 60. *Garden Pottery: Fluttering Bird bowl*

PLATE 61. *Garden Pottery: Swan by Gilbert*

PLATE 62. *Elephant bookends*

PLATE 63. *Danesby Ivory Pastel vases and bowl*

Although we have already mentioned that Fish bookends were produced as part of Denby's collection of fauna, it is interesting to note that they made their first appearance in the catalogues in the relatively rare Greenland series.

Ripple Ware

This formed part of the Danesby Ware collection but appeared to be an unpopular design. It is thought that only six different pieces were available in this fairly simply decorated series, which relied on a ridged finish for its appeal. All of the six pieces in the series were named, with no common thread linking them, except that they all began with the letter 'S', for example, Sherborne, Sheringham, Streatham, Sidmouth, and so on.

Herbaceous Border

This series appeared in the late 1930s; the extent of the range was more limited than some of the earlier Danesby Ware series, and the shapes were mainly taken from the Electric Blue and Orient Ware ranges, with the exception of No. 10, the Mackie jug, and No. 13, the Elgin bowl.

The decoration on the pieces is rather reminiscent of impressionist painting; the general background colour is a semi-matt, greyish glaze, with the 'floral' decoration (in lemon, green and blue), designed to give a hazy portrayal of an old-world cottage garden.

As with many of the Danesby Ware ranges, it is possible to find more individual pieces of Herbaceous Border which are not listed in the catalogues of the period; these are known to include lamp bases and larger 'one-off' vases.

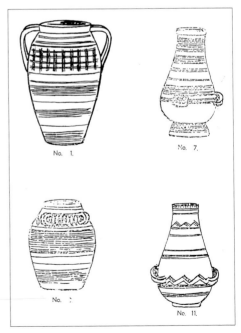

Folkweave

One of the most unusual of all the Danesby Ware ranges is Folkweave, probably introduced in the late

Figure 107. Some of the shapes available in the Folkweave design

114

1930s. It has an extraordinary coarse feel and appearance, rather like sandpaper. This is an actual matt glaze and not, as some people think, a textured finish. It is not dissimilar to a decorative glaze produced by the Poole Pottery earlier this century. The pottery has a light sandy base colour with bands in blue and darker brown, often with cross-hatching, and it is rather reminiscent of Samian Ware.

The shapes produced were catalogued by number – there were some thirteen in all. Many of the pottery pieces were quite large, being about 12 inches tall, and a large proportion were pitcher-type shapes (numbers 1, 3, 4, 5, 6, 10, 12 and 13). Numbers 7, 8 and 11 are more vase-like, but with rather interestingly-placed decorative handles and appendages, again reminiscent of the work of Alice Teichner (some of the shapes are illustrated in Figure 107). As with many of the Danesby Ware designs, there is a predominance of vases and jugs but very few bowl shapes. Number 9 in the Folkweave is the only bowl-shape that was produced – it takes the form of a rather large charger, some 13¼ inches in diameter. Again, look out for the unusual, non-catalogued items – one such piece is a tobacco jar (Plate 72).

Bulb Bowls

A varied collection of bulb bowls was added to the decorative ware catalogues in 1938, and it is interesting to note that they were advertised as Denby Ware and

Figure 108. Some of the bulb bowls available

LOMOND

LOTUS

ACTON

OWL

FLORAL

OVAL

PLATE 64. *Danesby Featherstone Ware (Regent Pastel glaze)*
(from left to right: Perth, Melville, Brailsford, Falkirk, Angus,
with Lanark bowl at the front)

PLATE 65. *Danesby Floral Pastel (from left to right – Back row: AT 39, Galloway,*
Kenmore, Forfar; Front row: Connel, Perth, Killin)

PLATE 66. *Tyrolean by Alice Teichner, in green and old gold glazes*

PLATE 67. *Tyrolean by Alice Teichner, in sepia and old gold, and green and sepia glazes – flower holders (AT 60/AT 59 [6 inches], AT 59 [8¾inches])*

Figure 109.
Bulb bowl –
Forres (blue
whirl)

not Danesby Ware. Many of the shapes were named after an assortment of geographical locations, such as Athol, Aviemore, Didsbury, Avon, Acton, Mundesley and Berkeley; some took their names either from their shapes or types of decoration, such as Square, Lily, Temple, Lotus, Owl and Floral. They were made in a wide variety of different glazes; sometimes one particular glaze was assigned to a particular named bowl, for example, Mundesley was only available in Oyster finish, Lomond in Cobblestone Green or Cobblestone Brown, and Didsbury in Mottled Blue or Copse decoration. Some of the range had relief-moulded decoration, not dissimilar to the Pastel ranges – the best examples are Oval (which features a faun and a tree), Owl and Floral.

PLATE 68. *Tyrolean by Alice Teichner, in sepia glaze – vase (AT 9), bowl (AT11)*

PLATE 69. *Tyrolean jugs and vases, and Puck ashtray in old gold glaze*
(from left to right: AT ?, AT 39, AT 32, AT 37, AT 31)

PLATE 70. *Collection of Denby Grey*

PLATE 71. *Danesby Herbaceous Border (from left to right: Brassington, Netherlea [8 inches], Elgon, Mackie, Netherlea [10 inches])*

PLATE 72. *Collection of Folkweave*

PLATE 73. *Large Denby Grey jug*

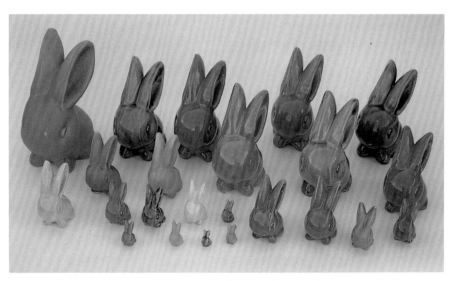

PLATE 74. *Marmaduke Rabbit Family*

121

16

Animals and Novelties

AT the height of Denby's production of art wares in the 1930s, a fascinating array of stoneware animals and novelties were made. The catalogues of this era list at least 80 different items, but some of these are extremely rare and hence difficult for collectors to find.

Rabbits

The most popular and easily obtainable are the broad-faced rabbits called Marmaduke. They made their first appearance around 1928–29 and were most probably modelled on a rabbit designed by Plichta which was produced at the Bovey Tracey Pottery.

They come in a variety of sizes: 00 (1¼ inches [3 cm]), 0 (1¾ inches [4½ cm]), 1 (3¼ inches [8 cm]), 2 (4½ inches [11 cm]), 2A (6 inches [15 cm]), 3 (8 inches [20 cm]) and 4 (9½ inches [24 cm]). The largest size was frequently used as doorstops! Sizes 2A and 00 are the most difficult to obtain as the former was added to the range at a later date as there was too big a jump in size between sizes 2 and 3; size 00 is mainly to be found on novelty ashtrays and lamp bases and, although they were obviously retailed separately, they were so small when produced that proportionately less have survived. Although many of the rabbits are unmarked, they are easily recognisable from ones by other makers, such as Shaw and Copestake (Sylvac), because of their more robust nature and heavier weight.

They come in a variety of coloured glazes, including green (both matt and glossy), pastel blue, glossy blue, yellow, buff, brown, cream and even pink (although the latter three are more uncommon). The most sought-after rabbits are those with the dark blue/purple/rust-coloured Orient Ware glaze; many collectors long to find one in the Electric Blue glaze, but we only know of one such example in a private collection. The brown rabbits almost certainly date from the early World War II years when production at the factory had to be mainly concentrated on domestic ware in a limited range of coloured glazes, namely brown, green and buff.

Production of rabbits did re-start after the war as the promotional information suggests, but their popularity had sadly declined on account of a depressed market for fancy and decorative goods. Most of the rabbits produced in the post-war period were in a cream-coloured glaze bearing the round Bourne Denby mark.

Figure 110. Post-war promotional material

WHO SAID "FREEDOM"?

Poor bunny has been penned up for five years. Not much longer now! Soon we're hoping to let him go and then he'll be finding his way into all the shops in the country. (There's a Benjamin and Peter and Flopsy Mopsy and Cotton-tail: the whole family in a range of colourful finishes.) Yes, Denby Art Ware is *really* coming back again.

DENBY *Ware*

JOSEPH BOURNE & SON LTD., DENBY POTTERY, NEAR DERBY

★

It is interesting to note that, after the War, when chocolate was scarce, some of the more affluent families bought Denby 'bunnies' for their children for Easter instead of the traditional Easter egg!

Some rabbits were made as cotton wool dispensers, having a circular hole instead of a tail; although these were made at the Denby factory, they were marketed by another company and are usually marked 'Cottontail' with a registered number.

Rabbits also appeared on ashtrays, of which there are two types – the Dainty and the Imps; they are also to be found on bookends and lamp bases. The rabbit lamp base is a delightful and collectable item in which the column is a tree trunk, around which is a group of three rabbits.

If you visit the Denby Pottery Museum, you will see in the display cabinets

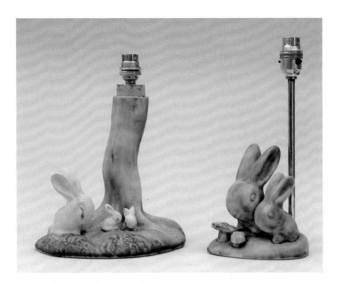

PLATE 75. *Danesby Ware – Rabbit lamp bases*

PLATE 76. *Danesby Sylvan Pastel Rabbit bookends*

PLATE 77. *Rabbit group in shiny blue glaze*

PLATE 78. *Group of Byngo dogs*

PLATE 79. *Danesby Pastel Blue Dog bookends, Terrier bookends, Scottie*

several lop-eared rabbits; it remains a mystery as to whether or not these were produced commercially in any quantities as they do not appear in any catalogues, nor have we ever seen any available for purchase. It is also interesting to note that similar lop-eared rabbits were originally made by the Bovey Tracey Pottery.

Dogs

Dogs feature strongly in the Denby stoneware menagerie – they appear in many different breeds, shapes and sizes, the most popular being a rather comical, but sad, French Bulldog called Byngo. He is easily recognisable by his dark-coloured left ear, and, like the rabbits, comes in a range of sizes: 0 (2 inches [5 cm]), 1 (2½ inches [6 cm]),

Figure 111. Large Scottie dog

2 (3¼ inches [8 cm]), 3 (7¼ inches [18 cm]), and 4 (9¼ inches [23 cm]). Unlike the rabbits, they were made in a much more limited range of coloured glazes – matt cream, glossy green, glossy brown, Regent Pastel and occasionally shiny blue.

The Byngo dogs also appeared on other novelty items, including the triangular-shaped Byngo ashtray and the Byngo dog bowl. The 1930s catalogue boasts no fewer than twelve other types of stoneware dogs, including Fido, Terrier, Puppy, Wire-Haired Terrier, Fox Hound, Paddy Terrier, Scottie, Dachshund, Buttons, Spaniel, Sammy. Many of these are extremely rare – such as Scottie, Spaniel, Fox Hound, Dachshund – and some appear on ashtrays, bookends and even finials on tobacco jars and marmalade jar covers. Sammy is also found on the Sammy dog bowl.

Fido is worthy of singling out.

Figure 112. Group of Terriers (designed by Alice Teichner)

Designed by Alice Teichner and produced in the Regent Pastel glaze, he was a rather comical, but sad-looking, figure and came in four different sizes: 0, 1, 2 and 3.

Figure 113. Group of Fidos

The Wire-Haired Terrier, although not the most attractive of modelled dogs, is certainly most interesting in that it rarely bears the Bourne Denby mark. Those that are marked frequently have the AT monogram (Alice Teichner – see mark V in the glossary of marks later in the book) and the words 'Made in England'. The terriers are modelled with an undulating surface, intended to simulate thick clumps of wiry fur. They were made in five different sizes (00, 0, 1, 2 and 3) and, like the Byngos and the rabbits, can also be found on bookends and ashtrays.

Lambs

Lambs were added to the novelties catalogue in the late 1930s and were obviously produced in large quantities as they can easily be purchased at antique markets and collectors' fairs; they come in seven different sizes, and usually three different varieties of glaze – pale green, cream and black – although other colours are known to exist. They are characterised by their cut-out eyes which, although

Figure 114. Denby's flock

PLATE 80. *Collection of dogs, including Terrier, Fido, Basket and Puppy ashtrays, Byngo, Dachshund and Sammy*

PLATE 81. *Danesby Pastel Geese group, Geese ashtray, Geese lamp base*

PLATE 82. *Novelties: Goose Family*

PLATE 83. *Frog and Cat*

Figure 115. Noah's Ark (taken from Denby's original 1930s promotional photograph)

quite appealing in the smaller sizes, can appear quite ghostly in the two largest sizes. Lambs too, like the rabbits, were also produced in the 'Cottontail' version, and also as ashtrays.

Other Animals

Although cats are very popular pets in Britain today, they do not feature very strongly in the Denby animals' section. A large cat was produced (Plate 83 and Figure 116), but there appears to be very few in existence. A smaller version, the kitten, was produced in a shiny black glaze, but these too are quite rare. According to the Denby catalogues there was a Cat serviette ring but we do not know of the existence of any examples.

Ducks and geese are well represented; as already mentioned, the geese were designed by Donald Gilbert. There are, however, different sizes: a small set (boxed) and large set (also boxed), as well as the large 14-inch high, Mother Goose. Two rather attractive ashtrays, called Goose and Gander, were also made, each one featuring three small models. Ducks, modelled as if they were swimming, came either singly, in five different sizes (the original prices varying between 4d. and 2/6d. [2p and 13p]!), or in a boxed set of four, called Duck Family. The ducks were produced in either a blue or green, semi-matt glaze. Also made was a set of

Figure 116. Cat

more comical-looking ducks, standing on a base, and a duck ashtray.

Pigs too, were made, although these are very rare indeed. These were produced in a cream-coloured glaze, with grey shaded areas; they could be purchased as a family of three (one large and two small), or singly, attached to an ashtray. However, by far the most amusing novelty was the Piggie ashtray, which was in the shape of a feeding trough with three pigs' rears being the main feature.

Other animals included an elephant, donkey (in three different sizes and in three different coloured glazes – green, black and grey), donkey and cart, and also a giraffe, which again was produced in several different sizes and colours. Another of the rarer items in the animal novelties was the teddy bear (Figure 117).

Figure 117. Teddy bear

Birds

Birds (other than ducks and geese) were very popular as novelties. In addition to the penguins already described, there was a penguin family, sold either singly or boxed, a penguin group on a rock, and a penguin ashtray. Other bird novelties included Birds Nest ashtray and Birds Nest spill vase, both of which featured two small birds sitting on the side of a nest-shaped pot, the texture of which simulated interwoven twigs. A rather comical item was the Chick fern pot which had an open-mouthed chick sitting on the edge of a pot, the outside of which resembled a tree trunk.

The list of ashtray novelties is seemingly endless (people must have been heavy smokers in the 1930s!); two more bird ashtrays are the Seagull and the Shell (this latter one featured a seagull too, but the bowl of the ashtray was in the shape of a shell). Three other bird novelties of note are the rather oddly-named Strident, and also the Bird and Flower and the Hen and Chicks.

Wall-mounted novelties included the Bird wall vase, and also a set of three Flying Ducks (very similar in size and colour to the Beswick ones, but of course made of stoneware). These could either be purchased as ornaments or as wall pockets, and were available in either a pale green glaze or multi-coloured (hand-decorated). We believe the production of the Flying Ducks was revived in the late 1950s when they were made in white earthenware (see the details in the

PLATE 84. *Novelties: Pigs and Giraffes*

PLATE 85. *Novelties: Birds and Flower plaque, and Bird wall vases*

PLATE 86. *Group of novelty ashtrays with Birds and Animals*

PLATE 87. *Flying Ducks*

section on New Glyn Ware in the chapter 'The Sixties').

Fish

The Fish bookends have already been described in the previous chapter on Danesby Ware and the designer Donald Gilbert. There were, however, one or two other fish novelties, all of which are sadly very rare. They include the Moray ashtray and Dundee bookends (see the section on Featherstone Ware in the previous chapter for further details); also Flying Fish, which was a wall-mounted ornament, and Dolphin ashtray.

Figured Novelties

There is a small, but interesting, collection of novelties (again, mainly ashtrays and spill vases), which feature different figures. These include the

Figure 118. Skier ashtray

Pixie Toadstool and Pixie Toadstool ashtray, both of which are delightfully modelled. Another ashtray in similar vein is the Puck ashtray which features the legendary character, Puck, sitting astride a log whilst being watched by a small rabbit (this piece was designed by Alice Teichner, and may well have the AT mark on the underside).

Other figured novelties include the Nipper ashtray and the Footballer ashtray, but the two most interesting and well-modelled ones are the Skier ashtray and the Caddie ashtray. A novel version of this golfing subject is the Caddie spill holder, in which the golf bag is the receptacle for holding the spills (Plate 89).

There is one more figured novelty worthy of note – the Boatman ashtray, in which the tray is in the shape of a boat, and the boatman is bedecked in gumboots and sou'wester.

As World War II approached and patriotic emotions were running high, three extra novelties were added to the catalogues; they were three ashtrays in the shape

Figure 119. Three military 'cap' ashtrays

of three different Services caps –
Air Force, Navy (catalogued
Sailor) and Army. There was also
a version of Byngo called ARP
Dog, in which he was wearing a
tin hat and had a 'wound' on his
flank which was marked with a
cross of 'sticking plaster'.

Several more novelties started
to be made circa 1938; these are
all very rare, as the onset of World
War II caused premature cessa-
tion of their production. The complete list is:

Figure 120. Fawn

1. Challenge ashtray, featuring a dachshund on one side and a bulldog on the other.
2. My Pals ashtray, featuring terrier dogs.
3. Countryside ashtray, having two small rabbits and two toadstools.
4. Toadstool spill can in which the centre of the toadstool is hollow for the storage of spills, and on the base is a goose and a small frog.
5. Fawn, in brown or cream.

Finally, before we leave the Denby novelties, a series of wall ornaments was introduced again circa 1938. These were flat, plaque-type pieces which were mainly aimed towards the children's market; they included Peter Pan (rabbit playing the flute), Prancing Horse, Goose Family, and Gambolling Lamb, and a rather odd, pottery-framed plaque, called Canterbury Bell plaque.

Figure 121. Grand Parade (taken from Denby's original 1930s promotional photograph)

135

PLATE 88. *Miscellaneous novelty group including Lop-Eared Rabbits, Fish, Squirrel, Panda (?), Duck, and Tree with Bluebird*

PLATE 89. *Caddy novelty spill holder*

PLATE 90. *Pixie Toadstool ashtray, Puck ashtray, Pixie Toadstool*

PLATE 91. *Nursery wall plaques:*
Prancing Horse, Gambolling Lamb, Peter Pan

PLATE 92. *Glyn Ware tankards*

PLATE 93. *Glyn Ware mugs and jugs*
(from left to right: Back row – Globe jug, Beer mug, Chalice, Goblet;
Front row – 701A [apparently un-named], Barrel jug, Swiss jug)

This text and illustrative evidence of Denby animals and novelties is by no means exhaustive; one of the exciting things about collecting these is that unusual and unique non-catalogued items are continually being found. One excellent example of this is the spill vase featuring the wire-haired terrier with the tree trunk on which is sitting a small cat (Figure 122).

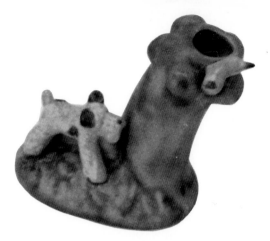

Figure 122. Spill vase featuring a wire-haired terrier and a small cat

Sadly the War intervened, and as the austerity measures began to take effect so the production of novelties ceased, with only the re-emergence of the Marmaduke Rabbits, and of course, latterly the novelty Frogs, being produced today.

17

The End of an Era

DANESBY WARE continued to be made into the first part of World War II but it is difficult to actually pinpoint accurately exact dates and production details between 1938 and 1942. It is almost certain that by this date the Electric Blue, Orient Ware, Regent Pastel and Pastel Blue had been discontinued.

The main influence on the designs at this time was Alice Teichner, whose work has already been described in some detail. The 1937 catalogue lists Redstone Ware as being produced; pots in this ware consisted of an unglazed, terracotta-style body, with a creamy-yellow glazed band at the top. Most of the wares made in this range were of a more functional nature, for example, jugs, toilet sets, vases and flower tubes, and bulb bowls.

Also listed was Denby Greenstone Ware which was a series of vases, jugs, plant pots, flower tubes and bowls in a rough-textured, matt green glaze. Several Danesby favourite shapes were used in this range including Crich, Netherlea, Brassington and Avon, but some new ones arrived on the scene, such as Clumber, Sheringham and Rufford. An interesting variation of the Netherlea was the Double Netherlea, which was really like a large flower tube with a bulbous section in the middle.

Farmstead and Gretna

These were two other ranges of 'plain' decorative wares which were introduced around 1938–39. Both these series shared the same shapes, many of which were totally new ones and had not previously been used in other Danesby Ware ranges. Gretna was produced in a light green semi-matt glaze with contrasting bands of dark green, and Farmstead had an overall cream glaze, with contrasting blue. The shapes

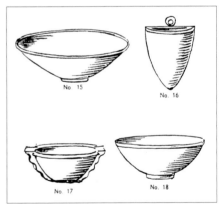

Figure 123. Some Farmstead/Gretna shapes

were not now given names but were merely identified in the catalogues as G1, G2 (G for Gretna), and F1, F2 (F for Farmstead), and so on. Some of the pieces were quite large (up to 13 inches and 14 inches high), and many of the vases had handles. Also included in the range was a 12½-inch diameter bowl (G15/F15), a wall pocket (G16/F16), and an ashtray (G17/F17). By June 1940 both Gretna and Farmstead had been withdrawn.

Figure 124. Gretna jug and vase

Old Ivory

This series, again a 'plain' decorative range, i.e., having just one overall glazed colour, was, as the name implies, an ivory colour (yellowy-cream). This series, too, was introduced around 1938–39 and the range of shapes available (although having certain similarities of style) was different from either Gretna or Farmstead. Again the shapes were identified in the catalogues just by numbers; only one or two had a resemblance to earlier Danesby Ware shapes, for example, No. 15 was the Hopton shape used in the Electric Blue and Orient Ware designs, and No. 19 was rather reminiscent of No. 8 in Folkweave.

Figure 125. Old Ivory shapes

Waverley

Another design produced towards the end of the 1930s, and whose production was curtailed by the War, was Waverley. This range could either be purchased in a cream-coloured glaze or a semi-matt green. Yet another new range of shapes were designed for this series, and again, the emphasis was on vases and bowls.

One design feature was that many of the vases and bowls had ornamentation

141

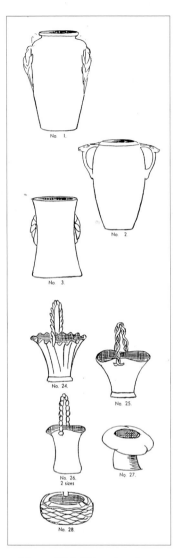

Figure 126. *Waverley shapes*

Figure 127. *Waverley Squirrel bowl*

on the handles in the form of animals' heads, ropework and scrolls, and many had scalloped edges. The production of the Waverley range did re-commence for a short time after World War II, around 1947.

Old English, Springtime Green, Tibet, Cottage

Another design of Danesby Ware was introduced most probably in 1938 or 1939. This was quite an extensive range of decorative ware, but sadly its popularity was only short-lived; it was discontinued in 1942. There was a large range of shapes available – several of the vases had twisted, rope-style handles and some of the larger bowl shapes were quite elegant, having fluted sides.

All the four different designs shared the same shapes; it was the variation in glazes and decorative features which made each different. The Tibet is certainly the most striking, having a satin-finish glaze with a colour flowing from donkey brown through to a dusty blue. Springtime Green, as the name implies, is a pale green colour with a semi-matt glazed finish. Old English has a silvery-grey semi-matt finish and could be purchased with or without the hand-painted floral decoration.

18

The Effects of Wartime

AS already stated, the onset of World War II caused a gradual scaling down of production of decorative art pottery. Obviously, demand for this type of pottery had naturally declined, but also wartime surcharges of 20 per cent had to be levied on most goods produced.

By the end of 1942, production of all but essential and functional pottery had finished. The factory still continued to make insulators, but the largest proportion of the output was for the Forces and therefore assisted the war effort – this included battery jars, jugs, plates, cups and saucers, cookware and, of course, NAAFI teapots!

'Bourne's List' for 1944 only comprised three pages. Very strict wartime regulations had to be adhered to, and the front cover reads 'This List contains full particulars of all the articles we are now permitted to manufacture and supply', and it was also noted that the 'London Office and Showroom are closed for the duration of the War'.

Cookware and hot water bottles therefore formed the mainstay of the production for the domestic market; glazes were limited mainly to browns, green and, of course, colourless. Pottery made at this time continued to be marked with a date and a reference to the monarchy (George VI) (see mark X in the glossary of marks later in the book).

Wartime regulations were still in effect in 1947, as the catalogue for this year was almost identical to the one from three years previous. However, in 1945, production of some decorative pottery was allowed, provided it was for export.

Tally-Ho

This pottery, based on earlier hunting jugs was made for the American market from 1945 to 1947. The range was developed by Albert Colledge, and consisted of tankards, mugs, jugs, goblets and tobacco jars. The main colours for Tally-Ho were mahogany brown top and bottom, with a central pale-green glazed band, to which were applied hunting scene 'sprigs'; on some pieces a windmill was applied, but it is interesting to note that they used the earlier 19th-century form with the cornfield dipping to the left. Although this pottery was made solely for export, amazingly there is quite a large amount in circulation in this country.

The Tally-Ho idea, however, was continued after 1947 and variations on this

Figure 128. Tally-Ho (from left to right: Old Man cider mug, greyhound-handled mug, antique cream jug with festive figures)

theme were produced for the home market until around 1952. The range was called Antique Ware which had a semi-matt lighter brown glaze top and bottom with an antique cream centre panel. Items produced in this included Stag jug, Gipsy jug, Tally-Ho mugs (that is, with the hunting scene in the centre panel), and Toby jugs.

Also produced in the Antique Finish were Hunting jugs in three different sizes, but most interesting are the Old Man cider jug and cider mug which have an applied 'sprig' featuring a rustic clutching a cider jug. Both of these pieces have gold lustre handles and bands to top and bottom. There was also a barrel-shaped tobacco jar made in this series, but to our knowledge this was never included in the catalogues.

Finally, also produced for the home market were teasets (comprising teapot, hot water jug, cream jug and sugar basin) in the antique cream semi-matt glaze; the 'sprigs' on these consisted of a Jacobean scene with people sitting around a table, eating and drinking. These teasets could be purchased with or without the gilded, gold lustre finish (evidence suggests that there has been very little gilding done in the whole of Denby Pottery's history).

The mark underneath pieces from the 1940s is, invariably, a circle inside which are the words Bourne, Denby, Derby, and outside of which is also 'Made in England' (see mark Y in the glossary of marks later in the book).

19

The Fifties

RESUMPTION of art pottery production at Denby after World War II began circa 1948 when the first studio was set up by Albert Colledge (who was partly responsible for the production of much of the 1930s art wares, as well as for the introduction of the ever-popular Greenwheat tableware design in the 1950s).

The Work of Glyn Colledge

Glyn Ware

Albert Colledge's son, Glyn, on his return from service in the Forces, joined his father in the design and decoration of the new hand-decorated stonewares and then, around 1950, took over the department to gain worthy recognition, not only for the production of Glyn Ware, but also for many other decorative designs as well as tableware. Glyn's family connections have a long pedigree going back to the earlier part of the 19th century; his great-great grandfather, William Coulton, worked at the Pottery in the early stages of its development, and his great grandfather invented a new lathe for making telegraph insulators in 1883.

It is interesting to note that the title Danesby Ware (which had always been associated with decorative stoneware), returned after the War and was in use until the early 1950s when it was eventually dropped in favour of the name Glyn Ware.

The words 'Made in England' are clearly visible on the underside of most pieces of Glyn Ware, but the main reason why the name 'Denby' does not appear is because individual, non-domestic, decorative items were not subject to purchase tax, provided that each one was individually signed. Hence, at the end of each day, Glyn Colledge had to sign each piece with his left hand, whilst holding it up in his right hand and whilst the slip was still wet! This helps to explain why the signature 'Glyn' is almost illegible (note that lamp bases were not generally signed as there was usually no base where the signature could be added).

There are many different shapes of Glyn Ware jugs, pitchers, dishes and bowls and many of these have specific names, such as Swiss jug, Persian jug, Arundel jug and Kenilworth jug; others are catalogued with much more ordinary-sounding names, such as Large jug, Chalice, Globe jug, Tankard, Goblet, and so on. Some of these shapes are illustrated in Plate 93; However, it is not uncommon to find 'one-off' or experimental shapes; one such known piece is a musical jug!

The main inspiration for the designs on Glyn Ware came from the eastern Mediterranean and Middle Eastern cultures and civilisations, particularly Italian, Persian and Byzantine.

The decorating department proper started in 1948 with a small group of existing workers (about eight) who, since the War, had been working with Albert Colledge. In addition to the existing decorators, several young women were set on,

Figure 129. Glyn Ware pictorial mug

one of whom was Audrey Jackson, a young 15-year-old, who was proud to follow in her grandfather's (William Jackson) footsteps, by working at the Pottery (his three sons also worked at Denby; all were saggar makers).

At the height of the production of Glyn Ware in the 1950s the number of paintresses had reached about 70. The 'girls' (as they were called) were initially taught three basic brush strokes which they practised until proficient; when they had gained the necessary confidence and experience, they were encouraged to use self-expression in colours, leaf and even floral decorations. Each paintress had her own identification mark, which took the form of a coloured spot, alongside Glyn's signature. The more collectable pieces of Glyn Ware have more imaginative and intricate decorations – these are likely to have been decorated by Audrey Jackson (black spot), Joan Baker (blue spot), Olga Gration (orange spot) and Veronica Wilson (brown spot). Other decorators included Joan Corbett, Sylvia Timmis, Gwen White, Audrey Annable, Kath Riley and Joan Blatherwick. If individual pieces have no spot at all, and are highly decorative with leaf and floral designs with very delicate tendrils, they may have been decorated by Glyn Colledge himself!

Although most Glyn Ware has a semi-matt glaze with leafy pattern designs, the rarest and most valuable pieces have a more shiny, transparent glaze, and have hunting, coaching and inn scenes painted on them; some of the larger pieces, such as lamp bases and pitchers, have painted scenes of yachts, sailing ships and even cathedrals.

Many of these more individual items of pottery were made for, and marketed in London by, a certain Mr Goodyear, who was, at the time, Court Florist and had a shop near to Clarence House. The inspiration for the hunting scenes (which were mainly painted by Audrey Jackson and Joan Corbett) came from a 19th century book about hunting, called *Jorrocks* in which some of the pictures were

PLATE 94. *Glyn Ware with hand-painted scenes: two fruit bowls with horses, and lamp base with Norfolk Broads scene*

PLATE 95. *Glyn Ware: Large jug (14 inches high), fruit dish (12½inches diam.)*

PLATE 96. *Glyn Ware: Jugs (from left to right: Kenilworth, Cider, Persian)*

PLATE 97. *Group of Cheviot vases, from 15 to 18 inches high*

PLATE 98. *Glyn Ware: Tankard and Cider jug with hand-painted hunting scenes*

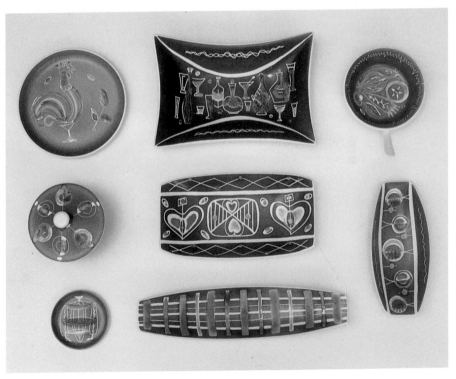

PLATE 99. *Selection of Cloisonné*

PLATE 100. *New Glyn Ware*

PLATE 101. *Glynbourne: hand-painted lamp bases*

almost cartoon-like. Mr Goodyear purchased some of the best Glyn Ware that was made, and particularly popular with his customers were cider sets, which consisted of a large straight-sided jug (with a large pouring lip), and six goblets, or small, handled mugs. Each piece was decorated with a hand-painted scene, the usual subjects being inns and hunting.

Other Glyn Colledge Designs

Glyn Colledge continued as Denby's leading designer throughout the 1950s and the 1960s. Although he is mainly recognised for Glyn Ware and Glynbourne (see the next chapter), there were many other decorative series designed by him in the 1950s.

Anyone who has visited Denby Pottery and has entered the video room, will certainly have noticed the tall and elegant vases which are displayed above the doorway. These belong to the **Cheviot** range and date from around 1957. Their shapes are very typical of 1950s art pottery and they display a variety of different glazes. Perhaps the most striking of these is the black with etched decoration, and also others similar but with a grey glaze. Also available in the range was a plain white, but there were also many other combinations – blue with black decoration, yellow with black, green with white, red with white, and purple with black. It is rare to find vases such as these for sale (there are some examples on display in the Victoria & Albert Museum in London); the tallest ones in the series are about 18 inches high.

Also produced in the Cheviot range and easier to find at antiques fairs and

Figure 130. Group of Cheviot vases

markets are bowls, dishes, trays and platters which all have very typical 1950s Deco shapes. These, like the tall vases, were produced in a variety of different contrasting colour combinations.

Cloisonné was another Glyn Colledge design which used the etching principle for the decoration. The basic overall glaze colour is charcoal grey with etched decoration (once again in typically 1950s Deco style), which is infilled with different coloured enamels – blue, red, yellow and lime green.

Designs on the various pieces range from abstract to fruit and vegetables, bottles and glasses, leaves, and people. The range was produced from 1958 to 1960 and was a limited series of decorative tableware including cruet, oil and vinegar bottle, egg set (comprising egg cup and plate), ramekin, egg poacher, coasters, and various shaped trays, dishes and bowls.

Figure 131.
Tapestry vase

Tapestry was a range of decorative pottery produced around 1957. The basic glaze colour to which the decoration was applied is matt white over which is a series of faint brown, vertical, textured lines (made to simulate fabric). Over this is overlaid stencilled leaf shapes – brown on green, and dark green on orange. There are seven different shapes available in the catalogues, whose names are linked geographically in that they are all the names of castles:

1. Glamis vase
2. Conway jug
3. Warwick vase
4. Windsor bowl
5. Richmond tray
6. Berkeley dish
7. Stirling dish.

Crystalline dates from around 1954 and was a series of decorative bowls, jugs, baskets, nut trays and sweet dishes. The basic off-white glaze has a 'crystalline' finish and the leaf decoration is in pastel colours. Figure 132 shows a two-handled vase (CL771).

Figure 132. Crystalline vase

Cretonne, like Crystalline, shares a similar range of pottery shapes and dates from around 1954. Again a white ground is used over which are bands of sponged red dappling together with stylised leaf and flower decorations.

There are many other facets of decorative Denby during the 1950s which admirably display the designs of Glyn Colledge. It is possible to find experimental pieces and other items of a more individual character. Of particular interest in this period are some dishes and trays, usually with a black ground and on which are tube-lined 'pictures'.

Other Decorative Pottery of the 1950s

It is very difficult to draw up a complete picture of all the decorative work done in the studios at this time. Some of the designs were only in production for a relatively short period; one such design is *Celadon* which was a series of different-shaped jugs, bowls, baskets and nut trays, which have a shiny-green glaze over which is slip-trailed basic wavy lines and leaf designs in the style of 18th century earthenware pottery decoration.

Figure 133. Celadon dish

The shapes in the *Cresta Ware* series are based on shells of different shapes and sizes, including conch, cornucopia, whelk, snail, winkle, and so on. They were copied from pearl-effect ware and were made primarily for flower-arranging; the famous 1950s flower arranger, Constance Spry, featured the ware in her pamphlet on the subject. The vases were available in a variety of different coloured glazes including green, lemon and white, often with a contrasting

Figure 134. Group of Cresta Ware vases

colour (such as red), inside. Cresta Ware dates from around 1950.

Hill-Ouston Ware was a limited range of pottery which was made for a local giftware wholesaler/retailer around 1955. The ornate moulded shapes have a basic semi-matt white glaze with applied floral decorations.

The **Ferndale** range of vases and bowls produced in the 1950s and the early 1960s is now becoming quite

Figure 135. Hill-Ouston vase

popular with collectors. The ware has a matt, pale-green glaze, with white swirls of decoration which resemble cake icing. A selection of items from this range are shown in Figure 136.

Tigo Ware pottery is especially noteworthy in that it is a most striking design. The first designs were launched in 1953, but it was not until 1954 that the whole range of small dishes and jars were marketed. Tibor Reich, of Hungarian descent, ran a company in Stratford-upon-Avon which specialised in texture weaving and in 1954 sponsored, in collaboration with two other companies, a travelling exhibition called 'Colour and Texture'. The basic idea of this exhibition was the

Figure 136. Group of Ferndale pieces

Figure 137. Tigo Ware including coffee pot, marrow vase and cream jug

Figure 138. Tigo Ware including Florence vase (first on left), cocoa mug and Clowns condiment set

use of black and white as a sharp contrast to colourful walls and furnishings. The black and white pottery created such great interest from its early development at Alderminster that commercial production of the wares was transferred to Denby Pottery, under the personal supervision of the designer.

The pottery has an ethnic appearance, and this is borne out by the names of some of the pieces, such as Madar Bird, Wuzu Bowl, Hajo Dish and Pusta Star. A fine collection of some of the more unusual pieces can be seen on display in the Denby Pottery Museum. Amongst the most attractive pieces which are eagerly sought-after by collectors, are Clowns condiment set, Sisters plate, Mustar condiment set, Rendezvous plate and the coffee pot and cocoa mug.

20

The Sixties

T HE year of 1958 was a turning point in the production of Glyn Ware. Unfortunately, analysis of working practices in the hand-decorating department at the pottery, revealed that some paintresses with more artistic flair were spending much longer than others on the decoration of individual pieces of Glyn Ware, but, in financial terms, the item would be retailed at the same price as an item which used fewer brush strokes and therefore took less time to produce. The survey resulted in more standardisation and stereotyping in future production; the 'girls' had to work to set patterns and there was no longer scope for free designs.

New Glyn Ware

Not only did New Glyn Ware have less intricate decoration, but also the pottery was made from white earthenware clay, which caused production problems when it was fired to stoneware temperatures in excess of 1,000 degrees centigrade. Usually, on the underside of each piece of New Glyn Ware is the

Denby mark (on some items the old 1940s/early 1950s circular mark is used, on others it is the traditional Denby scroll mark of the 1950s and 1960s), and also the signature of Glyn Colledge in full.

Glynbourne

The popular Glynbourne design was first introduced around 1960. Although this range of pottery is hand-decorated, the patterns are applied in a more controlled way than Glyn Ware. Apparently Glyn's wheel was sectioned off into sixths, and if you examine some of the Glynbourne vases closely, you will notice that there are six panels of decoration around the piece.

Figure 139. Glynbourne jug

There were fifteen different shapes of vases,

156

jugs, bowls and plant pots in the Glynbourne range; most of the designs use greens and browns, and the inspiration for the decorative motifs and ideas certainly comes from leaves and flowers.

The earliest pieces of Glynbourne usually have the signature, Glyn Colledge, incised in full on the base. However, it was discovered that this method of marking the bases of the pots was causing problems in the firing of the items. The incised mark was therefore superseded by an 'applied' signature to the unglazed base, together with the 1960s oval Bourne, Denby mark. However, in the final years of Glynbourne production in the early 1970s, Glyn's name disappeared altogether from the base of the pots, to be replaced by the 1970s rectangular Denby mark.

Figure 140. Reproduction William IVth flask with box

Although not catalogued, it is possible to find lamp bases in the Glynbourne style; these, of course, are rarely marked as they have no solid base. Before we leave the work of Glyn Colledge, it must be mentioned that this not really the end of the story. There was a lot of non-standard hand-decorating done at times when scheduled work was in short supply. Often plates, mugs and other items from the standard tableware ranges were hand-painted and sold through certain retail outlets. One collector is known to have a complete dinner and tea service made up of all different 'one-off' hand-decorated pieces!

Selected Designs and Ranges

In collecting terms, the 1960s (and 1970s) is fairly recent, but we have chosen to mention one or two selected areas which may be of interest.

Antique Reproductions

In an earlier chapter, we mentioned that reproduction reform cordial flasks were made primarily for the American market, during 1960–70. These were marketed in America by Milnor (a division of Denbyware Ltd), of Cincinnati, Ohio. As you

157

Figure 141.
Antique Repro-
ductions (from left
to right: Monkey
jug, Daisy jug,
Game dish,
Pistol, Toby jug

can see from Figure 140, the flasks were retailed in boxes which had the title 'Antique Reproductions', under which was printed 'Honored Mementos from Denby's Proud Heritage'. Six flasks were produced in the series which was extended to include other items 'for collectors, for gifts . . . as unique accessories'. These were re-created using the original moulds but using glazes which simulated salt-glazing. Some of the moulds, for example, Daniel O'Connell, had some of the features re-carved to produce crisper detail on the finished article. The only two of the original eight flasks described in chapter 2 which were not reproduced were Lord Grey and Peace. Some of these items are in circulation in this country, and so it is possible to purchase these at fairs and markets. The advertising material boasted that 'Denby Stoneware's modern technology produces the same intricate detailing and the same varying tones of brown and buff as Denby's famed original salt glaze kilns.' The range included Pistol spirit flask, Duchess of Kent flask (already described in chapter 5), Puzzle jug, Toby jug, Hunting mugs and jugs, Victorian vase, Daisy jug and Monkey jug. Some of these items are shown in Figure 141.

Village Stoneware

In a similar vein was the Village Stoneware range produced by the Pottery in the early 1960s and mainly

Figure 142. Village Stoneware – Handled casserole

aimed at the home market. The catalogues included the six flasks already described, but with slightly different glaze finishes. The rest of the items in the range were mainly functional, including stewpots, salad bowl, handled casseroles, coffee server and coffee mugs, teapot, cream jug and sugar basin, beer jug and beer

PLATE 102. *Glynbourne: five pieces including lamp base*

PLATE 103. *Glynbourne: three pieces*

PLATE 104. *Epic Green cookware, 1930s*

PLATE 105. *Selection of tableware designs*
(from left to right – Top row: Bokhara, Manor Green, Savoy, Arabesque;
Middle row – Gypsy, Greenwheat, Chevron, Ode;
Bottom row – Echo, Studio, Troubadour, Memories)

Figure 143. Flamstead shapes

mug, a salt shaker, pepper shaker and mustard, and also an oval game dish.

All these pieces have a simulated salt-glazed finish with darker brown tops and rims and all (except for the flasks) have relief-moulded 'sprigs' of windmills, trees, topers, smokers and hunters.

Flamstead

This range of decorative vases, jugs, bowls, trays and plant pots was introduced around 1967. The main feature of the design is a series of orange-coloured swirls in bands around the individual pieces. Figure 143 shows two of the thirteen items available.

Plant Pots

Around 1963, Denby introduced a range of plant pots in a variety of different decorative finishes. These included Ferndale, Combed (white on slate blue and white on Portland grey), Burlington (white on black), Grey Leaf (hand-painted leaf and flower in grey/green on matt white), Pear Drop (dark green on matt white), Spring (hand-painted leaf and bud on matt white), and Sun Flower (hand-painted decoration on glossy white).

Pop Singer

Denby Pottery has never been noted for producing figurines (apart from the few which appeared on the 1930s novelties). Stoneware is not a medium normally associated with figurines, but the pop singer in Figure 144 is very finely modelled and dates from around 1960.

Figure 144. Pop singer, circa 1960

21

Into the Seventies

WHEN we began to put together our book on Denby Stonewares, we decided that we would draw our conclusion around 1960. However, there are several particularly noteworthy production items which are eagerly sought after by collectors and thoroughly deserve a mention.

The Egyptian Collection

The 'Tutankhamen' plates were produced to coincide with the exhibition of artefacts which was held in 1972 at the British Museum. The set of four plates, called 'The Egyptian Collection' was the first and only series of limited edition collections of 'Ceramic Art through the Ages'. Five thousand sets of hand-decorated plates were made in Arabesque glazes; they were retailed in boxes of two, each set being numbered and having a scroll of authentication. The scenes on the plates were taken from a casket found in an antechamber of the King, with garlands, bouquets and plants from the same source. The titles of the plates were:

1. The King's Fisherman
2. The Queen's Handmaiden
3. King Tutankhamen
4. Queen Ankhesanamun.

Figure 145. Four Tutankhamen plates

Denby Village

Around 1975–76, Denby produced a set of four delightful hand-crafted, hand-painted stoneware replica cottages and houses. The four in the series were:

1. Cotswold Stone Cottage, typically found in Gloucestershire, dating back to the 16th century.

Figure 146. Denby Village – original promotional photograph

2. Thatched Cruck Cottage, some 600 years old, still found in the Midlands, particularly in Herefordshire.
3. Cumbrian Farmhouse, dating from the early 19th century, of rough cast stone, plastered over and painted white as a protection against the elements.
4. Georgian Town House, typical of those found in London and the South-West, dating from the late 18th century, built of brick and having a classic façade.

Finally, we must mention the work of two employees of the 1970s. At a time when there was less emphasis on art-style pottery, it is worth noting that one or two distinctive styles came from Denby at this time.

Figure 148. Studio-type vase by David Yorath, circa 1972

Figure 147.
Minaret vase

Firstly, a series of hand-decorated vases and other items, including ashtrays, was produced, usually with a toffee-brown base colour, and given an oriental flavour by the parallel bands of decoration in green, orange and turquoise blue. One hand-decorator of this ware, called Minaret (Figure 147), was Audrey Cole-Parker, whose initials ACP can be seen on unglazed bases.

Secondly, the studio-style pottery illustrated in Figure 148 was produced by David Yorath; this piece bears a close resemblance to certain pieces of Poole pottery of a similar period. There is an incised name YORATH in capital letters on the underside and an unusual incised DENBY mark, also in capital letters.

22

Tableware

NO book on Denby stoneware would be complete without reference to its main stock-in-trade which, of course, is the high quality tableware which has been produced over the decades.

In the late 1920s came the Cottage Blue design, which was a deep blue glaze on the outside, with a mustard-colour on the inside. This design was really Denby's first successful venture into general domestic lines and signalled a move away from being largely a producer of industrial ware.

The emergence of the designer Donald Gilbert, in the early 1930s, led to the development of two more distinctive ranges of tableware – Epic and Manor Green. The latter design was so popular that it continued to be made (along with Cottage Blue) until 1982! The advantage that stoneware had over earthenware and china was, that it was oven to tableware, which of course is a very important marketing feature to this day.

Epic was proudly advertised as 'Designs of Distinction' and was produced in a green glaze with a rich cream lining with a distinctive wave-like design in relief. An important selling point was that it could be used for cooking and then brought straight to the table for serving the food.

A similar series of oven to tableware, also designed by Donald Gilbert in the early 1930s, was Blue Cone Ware, which consisted of a cream background with a decoration of blue lines and a motif of the blue cone. This range, as with Epic, consisted of casseroles, oval entrée dishes, saucepans, baking dishes, hors d'oeuvres sets, jugs, cruets, coffee pots and teapots.

World War II caused ranges such as these to be discontinued as restrictions were placed on manufacturing industries. Production had to be limited to one main range called Utility Brown, which was dark brown on the outside and stone colour inside. Pieces from this period frequently do not bear the name Denby, but often have either 'Made in England' or just the one word 'Stoneware'.

After the War, the designs of Manor Green and Cottage Blue were re-introduced along with a new design called Homestead Brown, which had the dark brown outside (similar to Utility Brown) but with a light blue inside. All three of these designs, although discontinued, are still extremely popular with collectors today.

The 1950s saw the dawning of a new era in decorative stoneware tableware, and it was Denby Pottery which was the pioneer in this field. Albert Colledge

Figure 149. Ceramic palette advertising Denby Greenwheat – 1950s

and his son Glyn produced a succession of very popular, imaginatively designed oven to tableware ranges, which were soon to become household names. Firstly came Peasant Ware, but the most notable of all was the timeless Greenwheat design. This pottery was exported all over the world, and was particularly popular in the USA as well as Australia and New Zealand. This pottery, although it has been discontinued for two decades, is still extremely popular with collectors, and is still in use in many households.

No two pieces are identical, as the pottery was hand-crafted and hand-painted. The decorating was done by a team of paintresses; six 'girls' each added a part to the wheatear design on each item of pottery. The Greenwheat range was first introduced in 1955–56 and was finally discontinued in 1976.

Some of the earlier pieces of the Greenwheat range are more individual, and now quite rare; these include a cheese dish with a wedge-shaped lid on a teak base, a set of four egg cups on a teak stand, a cruet set (also on a teak stand), and sugar basins with teak lids.

Other popular tableware designs from the 1960s include Chevron and also the very distinctive Arabesque (introduced in 1964). Both of these ranges were designed by Gill Pemberton; the latter was originally named Samarkand. Arabesque, like Greenwheat, is still sought after today and some of the earlier pieces are becoming quite rare, such as covered canisters and jars, egg set with salt pourer on a tray, large tureen with teak stand, roasting dish with teak stand, goblets, colonel mugs, hors d'oeuvres dishes with teak stand, chop platter (14-inch diameter) and ice bucket. All of the items were hand-decorated, and the design proved so popular that it was not discontinued until 1984.

It is difficult to single out specific tableware designs as there have been scores of very successful ones over the last 45 years, but some of the more popular and easily-recognisable ones are illustrated in Plate 105; these include Studio, Echo, Ode, Bokhara, Troubadour and Gypsy.

Glossary of Pottery Marks

THE following list of marks will serve as a guide to the identification and dating of various pieces. As already stated, a proportion of the wares produced at Denby Pottery bear no marks at all; such examples have to be identified through recognition of shape, decorative features, and so on. All dates quoted are only approximate and some overlap between different periods does exist.

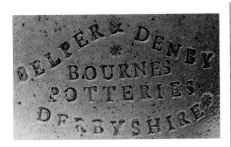

A – *c.1832*
Impressed on back of reform flasks

B – *c.1833+*
Impressed on back of reform flasks

C – *c.1840–50*
Impressed near base of bottles and jars (there are several different minor variations of this type of mark)

D – *c.1860–70*
Impressed near base of bottles and jars

E – *c.1880*
Impressed near base of bottles and jars

F – *c.1890*
Impressed near base of bottles and jars

G – *1890s?*
Rare impressed mark near base of ginger beer bottles

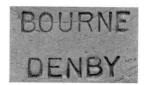

H – *Late 1880s*
Typically found impressed on bases of Victoria's Golden Jubilee commemoratives (along with Reg. No. 49901)

I – *c.1895–1900*
Most typically found impressed on bases of Victoria's Diamond Jubilee commemoratives

J – *c.1895–1900*
Rare impressed mark found on base of art pottery pieces (this mark was also used by Elliott on pottery from other factories)

K – *c.1895–1900*
Rare impressed mark found on base of art pottery pieces (usually with blue sgraffito decoration)

L – *c. 1890–1910*
Impressed base mark found on Majolica

M – *c.1899–1949*
Impressed mark near base of bottles (there are several variations, including a letter instead of a number; also a plain centre with no number or letter)

N – *c.1900–08*
Rare impressed mark near base of bottles

O – *c.1900–20*
Stencilled lettering on base

P – *c.1915–20*
Stencilled lettering on base

Q – *c.1920–25*
Impressed mark on base

R – *c.1920s*
Stencilled lettering on base

S – *c.1930–35*
Stencilled lettering mark found on both domestic and decorative wares

T – *c.1930–41*
Script stencilled lettering on decorative wares (used in conjunction with mark S)

U – *c.1935–50*

Stencilled lettering found mainly on domestic ware but also seen on later Danesby Ware

V – *c.1936–41*

Underglazed monogram used by Alice Teichner on decorative wares

W – *c.1937–38*

Rare underglazed script mark (used in conjunction with mark V)

X – *c.1940–45*

Stencilled lettering used during wartime (often dated and with reference to the monarch as a large proportion of the production was for the supplying of pottery to the Forces)

Y – *c.1944–50*

Stencilled lettering on base (often underglazed)

Z – *c.1948–58*

Underglazed signature Glyn (Glyn Colledge), usually found in conjunction with the words 'Made in England' – found on hand-decorated art wares

AA – *c.1950–74*

Stencilled mark on base (often underglazed) – usually found on domestic wares

DD – *1960s*

Impressed and/or stencilled underglazed mark found mainly on decorative wares

BB – *c.1956–76*

Stencilled lettering mark found on the base of the very popular hand-decorated Greenwheat range, and also bearing the name of the designer A College (the name is normally spelt with a 'd' between the 'e' and the 'g'). There are other variations of this Greenwheat mark

EE – *1974–early 1980s*

Stencilled mark on base of domestic tableware

FF – *1980s*

A base mark found on tableware, cookware and giftware of the period

CC – *c.1958–early 1960s*

Glyn Colledge's signature in full as used on New Glyn Ware – used in conjunction with the stencilled mark which is a variant of mark Y

GG – *1980s*

A base mark found on tableware, cookware and giftware of the period

HH – *1980s*

A base mark found on tableware, cookware and giftware of the period

Inspection of the bases of domestic and decorative wares produced by Denby over the years will reveal that, in addition to the marks illustrated in this glossary, there are other impressed marks; these often take the form of single letters as shown in the illustration below. This mark, and others like it, is the turners mark or figureman's mark (the figureman was the person who attached spouts and handles to the pot). This subject of impressed marks is a very complex one, because when one craftsman retired or moved on, his mark (letter) was passed to an apprentice who then adopted it to use as his own mark. Sadly there are no records in existence which allow us the privilege of being able to identify the names of the turners and figuremen, either at the turn of the century or in the heyday of decorative production in the 1930s.

The following very brief and incomplete information lists some of the craftsmen (and their marks) in the late 1930s, 1940s and early 1950s:

Craftsman	Mark
Albert Blancheon	B
Ebby Cartwright	
Arthur Eyre	
Joe Fletcher	J
Stan Fletcher	S
Sid Hislop	Z
Jack Lingard	H
John Lingard (son)	L
Ralph Oldknow	
Cyril Parkin	
Hedley Parkin	
(chief mould-maker)	

Example of impressed single letter mark used by turners and figuremen

As a general rule, it would appear that the earlier letters of the alphabet represented the turners, and the later letters the figuremen.

Index

(Page numbers in italic refer to colour illustrations)

Graham and Alva Key operate a China Matching Agency for discontinued Denby tableware produced between the early 1950s and the most recent discontinued patterns. This service has now been expanded to cover all Denby collectables, and they will search for your missing rabbits, dogs, vases, bowls, kitchenalia, and so on. If you would like to make use of their service they can be contacted by telephone or fax on (01785) 256648, or by writing to PO Box 387, STAFFORD, ST16 3FG